Understanding Azure Monitoring

Includes IaaS and PaaS Scenarios

Bapi Chakraborty

Shijimol Ambi Karthikeyan

Apress®

Understanding Azure Monitoring: Includes IaaS and PaaS Scenarios

Bapi Chakraborty
Bangalore, India

Shijimol Ambi Karthikeyan
Bangalore, India

ISBN-13 (pbk): 978-1-4842-5129-4
https://doi.org/10.1007/978-1-4842-5130-0

ISBN-13 (electronic): 978-1-4842-5130-0

Managing Director, Apress Media LLC: Welmoed Spahr
Acquisitions Editor: Smriti Srivastava
Development Editor: Matthew Moodie
Coordinating Editor: Shrikant Vishwakarma

Cover designed by eStudioCalamar

Cover image designed by Freepik (www.freepik.com)

Distributed to the book trade worldwide by Springer Science+Business Media New York, 233 Spring Street, 6th Floor, New York, NY 10013. Phone 1-800-SPRINGER, fax (201) 348-4505, e-mail orders-ny@springer-sbm.com, or visit www.springeronline.com. Apress Media, LLC is a California LLC and the sole member (owner) is Springer Science + Business Media Finance Inc (SSBM Finance Inc). SSBM Finance Inc is a **Delaware** corporation.

For information on translations, please e-mail rights@apress.com, or visit http://www.apress.com/rights-permissions.

Apress titles may be purchased in bulk for academic, corporate, or promotional use. eBook versions and licenses are also available for most titles. For more information, reference our Print and eBook Bulk Sales web page at http://www.apress.com/bulk-sales.

Any source code or other supplementary material referenced by the author in this book is available to readers on GitHub via the book's product page, located at www.apress.com/978-1-4842-5129-4. For more detailed information, please visit http://www.apress.com/source-code.

Printed on acid-free paper

Table of Contents

About the Authors

Bapi Chakraborty has over 14 years of IT experience in the field of on-premises and cloud infrastructure architecture, solution design, migration, deployment, and support practices. He has worked with customers and partners from various industries and understands their unique demands and requirements in order to achieve business goals. Bapi holds various industry and product certifications, including Microsoft, AWS, and IASA.

Shijimol Ambi Karthikeyan is a solutions architect with 13+ years' experience in IT and specializes in datacenter management, virtualization, and cloud computing technologies. She started her career with EY IT services in the datacenter management team managing complex virtualized production datacenters. She has expertise in managing VMware and Hyper-V virtualization stacks and Windows/Linux server technologies. She has also worked on DevOps and CI/CD implementation She later moved on to cloud computing and gained expertise in Windows Azure, focusing on Azure IaaS, backup/DR, and automation. She holds industry and product certifications including Microsoft, VMware, ITIL, and TOGAF9.

About the Technical Reviewer

Devendra G Asane is currently working as a Cloud, Big Data, and Microservices Architect with Persistent Systems. Prior to this, he worked with Microsoft.

Devendra lives with wife Seema and son Teerthank in Pune, India.

See his complete profile on `www.linkedin.com/in/devendra007`.

Acknowledgments

Bapi Chakraborty

I would like to thank my parents for their blessings and support
for everything that I have achieved in my life. Their teachings and
encouragement always help me to take up new challenges and not to fear
any failure through the journey of life.

My heartful thanks go to my wife, Maninder, who is always by my
side supporting me at every step. My two divine angels, son Shouvik and
daughter Ananya, always bring new perspectives in life, understanding my
unavailability and at times, asking questions that make me think how
I can explain concepts in an easier way.

Shijimol, my co-author, enabled us to drive this effort together. Most
importantly, she had faith in the idea and extended great collaboration
without which this book may not have seen the light.

Sincere thanks to the Apress team for their support, guidance, and
assistance during the entire process.

Shijimol Ambi Karthikeyan

First and foremost, I would like to thank my parents for everything
I have ever accomplished in my life, including this book. My mother,
Ambi R., always inspired me to work toward my goals no matter how
unrealistic others perceived them to be. My father, Karthikeyan M., taught
me that it is equally important to slow down at times and take in life as it is.
They are no longer around, but their love and blessings keep me going.

My husband, Sujai Sugathan, supported me throughout this endeavor
like he always does for all my adventures. My daughter Sanjana Sujai,
the sweetheart she is, gracefully put up with my absenteeism while I was
busy authoring the book. I am grateful for the support I get from my sister

ACKNOWLEDGMENTS

Gigimol A.K. and family, my best friend Anjana, my in-laws, and my extended family. Extending my thanks to Bapi, for being such a wonderful colleague and co-author. This book is his brainchild, and I am honored that he gave me an opportunity to contribute and collaborate. I am thankful to the mentors in my professional life – there are too many to list – for their constant support and encouragement. Last but not least, I would like to thank the entire team at Apress for their support during the publishing process.

Introduction

Microsoft Azure is one of the preferred cloud service providers today for a large number of organizations across various industries. The increase in cloud adoption has changed the way that organizations and IT professionals look at security, monitoring, and operational activities of IT resources. Effective monitoring helps become proactive to incident response management, increase operational efficiency, and positively impact security posture. This book will act as a guide for IT professionals, consultants, architects, and Azure administrators to understand the various aspects of Monitoring Azure infrastructure and applications.

We start with a mild introduction into the ever-changing world of various industries and how they are adopting the cloud and trying to understand how to monitor the new services. This book is authored to introduce the fundamental building blocks of monitoring the Azure Monitoring constructs, capabilities, and life cycle. It then dives into various scenarios of "cloud-only" and "hybrid" application monitoring. Then we will identify and create all the possible and crucial components required to design, architect, and implement strong robust monitoring solutions.

The reader will have a chance to explore and understand the various architectural constructs of Azure monitoring capabilities and how it can be leveraged by an enterprise and used by IT professionals to respond to the growing operational and security requirements in the cloud. Also, we will explain the integration capabilities with existing Security Information and Event Management systems for organizations implementing hybrid architectures on Azure.

CHAPTER 1

The Ever-Changing Landscape of the Cloud

When we conceived the idea of this book, we first wanted to ensure that you have a high-level view of how cloud technologies have changed and disrupted various industries in the recent past. The latest innovation in technology, "the Cloud," has changed things for good. Various organizations big and small are impacted and have been forced to adopt and include cloud technologies as part of their modernization strategy. No matter how big or small your organization is, which technology or product you use, and how you use it, you need to know what is happening in your environment, which triggers or events are important, and when and how you should react. Effective monitoring of the environment helps you achieve that. Monitoring is just not a collection of a few steps or actions; it is a complete process on its own that is unique to each organization and business. This is a cloud adoption and digital modernization journey.

The digital modernization journey can be both exhilarating as well as exhausting for enterprises as there are many moving parts to be taken care of during cloud adoption. This includes but is not limited to migration considerations, security, resiliency, high availability, and monitoring.

© Bapi Chakraborty and Shijimol Ambi Karthikeyan 2019
B. Chakraborty and S. A. Karthikeyan, *Understanding Azure Monitoring*,
https://doi.org/10.1007/978-1-4842-5130-0_1

For most organizations, the landscape is often hybrid, where some crucial application components remain on-premises during the initial phases while other tiers of the architecture are moved to the cloud. Stitching these components together in the monitoring layer often becomes a challenge, especially with the multitude of monitoring tools available in the market, both cloud native as well as third party. This book will attempt to cover the various architectural constructs of Azure monitoring capabilities and how it can be leveraged by an enterprise to respond to the growing operational and security requirements in the cloud.

In this chapter, we will quickly touch upon how public cloud computing changing the operational aspects of modern enterprises – those who have adopted, those who are born in the cloud, and those who are still strategizing and identifying what works for them and what doesn't. In each case, they need to identify how things change to be in a fully functional operationalization state.

The Traditional and the New

Let's look at how various industries and organizations at various maturity levels look at public cloud technologies.

Any change is complex and complicated. It is a process and cannot be achieved overnight. The same applies to cloud journey for digital modernization as well. Today, in every industry, many companies have accepted the need for cloud technology adoption. Based on the maturity level of the organization, they are looking to invest and innovate in always available, economical, resilient cloud infrastructure. Let us now look at how various industries, based on their scale of operation, are adopting the cloud and why.

Start-ups: They are the happiest segment to adopt the cloud technologies, the main reason being that there is no upfront capital expenditure. Most cloud providers offer a "pay-as-you-go" model in which you pay only for what you consume and only incur operational expenses. You will not be investing your money in an asset that you do not know how long you would really use. Furthermore, based on your usage, you can easily add or reduce resources and so you eventually pay less. Additionally, you do not need to hire someone to plan or procure any resources; it's just out there, and you can start consuming at the click of a button. This not only helps to reduce the risk of capital investment but also protects from unfortunate loss in case of venture failure.

Mid-sized organizations: This segment still can move quickly comparatively to the giant enterprises who have a lot of restrictions due to their scale of operations. They would like to innovate quickly, while also spending less time and effort to re-create an environment and restart experimentation again. At the same time, they would like to expand operations to new countries, regions, or reach out to new consumer segments, etc., making cloud technologies their best bet. The new age cloud technologies enable them to expand and effectively use resources and reduce costs and, at the same time, attain higher security compliance and governance. Exploring new markets and consumer segments or launching new product lines or categories become much easier.

Enterprises: Out of several challenges, the most prominent one for the modern enterprises is to maintain continuous growth without hurting any existing customer base or market. While the competition is very steep with several giant enterprises competing with each other in the same industry, it has pushed them to adopt a place to achieve higher resiliency, improved experimentation, security and compliance, hyperscalability, and quicker launch cycles of products to stay ahead of the competition. They are also well placed to introduce a good bargain in terms of pricing and contracting with the cloud vendor, owing to the sheer scale of operation and consumption.

Now let us look at some of familiar industries and how they are adopting the cloud and what parameters they look at while choosing a cloud vendor.

Banking, finance, and insurance: If you speak to any bank or insurance organization, the first word they would utter is "Security," the second is "Compliance," then everything else can follow. Of course, for obvious reasons, gaining trust in someone else's premises takes a while to grow, especially when you are dealing with someone else's money and keeping all information on someone else's platform. The adoption has been slow but it's gaining momentum for specific operations. For example, every bank wants to engage their customer effectively, keep an open communication mechanism, innovate on their products, and reach out to more customers. While the same holds true for the insurance sector, they also would like to run risk profiling and huge queries against millions of customer records before providing any loan or insurance. The advent of FinTech companies made competition more tough. Unlike any traditional banks, FinTech companies are leveraging cloud tools/ technologies like big data analytics, blockchain, machine learning to learn consumer behavior, much faster loan approval processes, and live customer interaction with video conferencing, etc. These have been disrupting the industry as a whole, opening up new avenues and changing how this sector used to operate. Among all these, to maintain the security posture, they need to know "what," "when," "how," "who," "where" of any event and its impact; they need a strong monitoring mechanism of every service they use and deploy.

Retail: Like banking, finance, and insurance, security, customer engagement and availability of the platform are the core aspects that the retail industry looks for while selecting a cloud platform. In terms of other priorities, these include providing the latest, freshest, and greatest customer experience, using an interactive platform that can provide a wide variety of choices, the capability to integrate with other service providers (e.g., banks and payment gateways) for loan processing and secure online payment. We notice the adoption of the cloud in this industry is faster since the very nature of the cloud platform being hyperscale, creating global presence in a minimal time frame, quicker onboarding, and the ability to reach out to customers from other countries at a very reduced cost. It reduces the capital investments on IT assets in other countries. You can now deploy a website in minutes without having to create any virtual machines, build a network infrastructure, and upload your product catalogue.

Media and advertising: Exabytes of data, large-sized files, formatting, encoding-decoding, and delivering them in various forms and sizes of devices are the core operations involved in this industry. Hyperscale processing, availability in minutes, and the capability of serving a global customer base are the key demands of this industry. At the same time, when to scale; what went wrong, when; and preventive measures to be taken are the key metrics the organizations need to know.

Manufacturing, oil and gas: These were a little late into the cloud adoption until IoT (Internet of Things) picked up the pace. The processes in HR, supply chain, customer engagement, CRM systems, etc., were among the early to onboard. Embedding some of the special chips into the actual manufacturing devices was the difficult part. Predictive maintenance, predictability in terms of quantitative outputs, and ensuring greater quality are the key drivers to move to the cloud. Whether it is deep sea exploration; or identifying and researching the quality of oil in the rocks, which requires high performance computing, new age computing has it all to serve this industry to the fullest.

On similar lines, we have health care, engineering and software, education, and so many more industries that have key requirements and reasons for choosing a cloud-based solution. At the same time, monitoring all the services hosted and making sure appropriate processes and tools are in place to handle any security and non-security events are key to its success. Microsoft Azure, being one of many cloud services providers, does just that. Let's us now look further into Microsoft Azure and see how it can help achieve key business objectives.

Microsoft Azure as a Strategic Choice

There are several public cloud service providers, and among them we have a few that really stand out: Amazon Web Services (AWS), Microsoft Azure, Google, Oracle, IBM, and Alibaba Cloud. It is always a matter of debate and discussion of which one is better? Who has better services for a lesser price? Who can satisfy my need better and generate value for me? And there are so many similar questions. While each of these service providers has similar services and certain times, each one is better than the other in certain ways, the main question that matters to most of the customers is which one can meet my requirements better and become a partner in my transformation journey?

As an architect, it will always be difficult to choose one over the other in terms of value; as a consultant or seller, there will always be a way to compare and contrast the features and capabilities. However, we all know that for one reason or other, we can always find the most suitable one that can meet our requirements and provide better value for our money. In the context of this particular book, let us look at some of these aspects specific to Azure before we dive deep in to the monitoring pieces. The items discussed next set the context of the capabilities that we will explore in upcoming chapters as well.

Decades of experience: Microsoft has been a leading software and services provider over the last three decades. Although it is one of the best choices in the enterprise segment, it has very good focus and presence for the middle and small businesses too. Its existing ISV ecosystem and strong and innovative services development have been able to deliver what is expected of them. This is why, as of today, Microsoft Azure serves more than 95% of the Fortune 500 companies. Enterprises trust Microsoft Azure.

Company focus and growth: The company has been investing heavily into the development of cloud-based technologies and product areas like blockchain, cybersecurity, IoT, containers, virtual reality, artificial intelligence, gaming, privacy, and security. In recent news, Microsoft stated that it will invest $5 billion globally in IoT over the next four years. News from January 2017 stated that Microsoft will continue to invest over $1 billion a year on cybersecurity. Its commitment to the common good – "Cloud for Global Good" is a page that you must visit to know more about Microsoft's policy road map: https://news.microsoft.com/cloudforgood/.

Global presence: Per recent data and information on Microsoft's website, its Azure services are available in over 140 countries, 54 regions worldwide, and up to 1.6 Pbps of bandwidth in a region – more than 130 edge node locations and 70,000 miles of fiber and undersea cable systems. These figures ensure its dominance in any country to serve the customer and stay close to them.

Wide partner network: Microsoft is well known for working with partners and reaching out to a larger customer base. It has a very wide range of partner programs that helps partners to leverage the new business opportunities in the cloud world through tools, resources, training, presales technical help, and best practices to grow their business. At the same time, they help to build necessary capabilities for Microsoft Azure and show to use it to their advantage. Microsoft reportedly has more than 64,000 cloud partners with various competencies – more than AWS, Google, and Salesforce combined.

Focus on open source: Microsoft has extended its Azure platform to support most open source languages, operating systems, tools, and frameworks. Microsoft recently acquired GitHub wherein it shares APIs, SDKs, and several open source projects, for example, Visual Studio Code, .Net, and TypeScript where Microsoft developers contribute every day. It's a must to visit: https://github.com/Azure. For open source releases, visit: https://opensource.microsoft.com/. Microsoft Azure supports an extremely broad selection of programming languages and tools, such as: .NET Framework, Node.js, PHP, Python, Ruby, Java, and more. Microsoft Azure fully supports hosting Linux virtual machines. In fact, 25% of Virtual Machines running on Microsoft Azure are running a distribution of Linux.

Hybrid cloud: Microsoft Azure can be easily used as an extended datacenter for its customers. Every customer wants to experience, test, and then host their workload on Azure. Once they are happy and satisfied with its services and capabilities, that is when the first step to migration is taken. Microsoft Azure can be integrated with an on-premises datacenters and branch offices with VPN connectivity, ExpressRoute, and Azure WAN. With such integration, an application can be deployed on Azure and at the same time can leverage all on-premises resources. An integrated monitoring and security posture can also be implemented across the IT assets, deployments, and ensure governance. For a true hybrid cloud experience, customers and partners can leverage Azure stack for similar Azure-like experiences on-premises. It's also worth mentioning the fact that since both Azure Stack and Azure leverage the same architecture, the same application once deployed can easily be ported or migrated from Azure to on-premises or the other way around without having to make any application changes. This is a huge win for customers.

Strong support and services system: Microsoft is well known for its support and consulting services. It has an established process and support model to help the customer when required, based on 24x7x365 days and critically based SLAs.

Given some of the core factors as discussed, Microsoft Azure is a strategic choice for customers, and we see good case studies of digital transformation in various industries. Visit `https://azure.microsoft.com/en-in/case-studies/` for more details.

The Multi-Cloud Strategy

With the higher adoption of cloud, most organizations prefer to adopt a multi-cloud strategy to host their application. This is due to various reasons, including breaking provider dependency, increasing reliability, better cost negotiation, reducing the attack surface, adopting a development model that fits across cloud deployment, and a safe datacenter exit strategy. Deciding a strategy is one challenge and implementing it is another. Operationalization and monitoring across the cloud and having visibility of end-to-end deployment is a difficult task to achieve without the right set of tools and methods. At times, the same monitoring tool may not be sufficient for the needs and requirements to be used to integrate with other tools to achieve the required goals. Hence, choosing the right tool for your needs is absolutely important for multi-cloud strategy success.

Operationalization and Learning Curve

The cloud adoption journey starts with an envisioning phase where an enterprise cloud adoption strategy is defined. The vision and scope should be clear and well defined to give the organization a sense of direction. While there is a huge demand for a cloud-first approach for new applications, transformation of existing applications could result in a hybrid architecture. In both approaches, cloud adoption moves through the cycle shown in Figure 1-1.

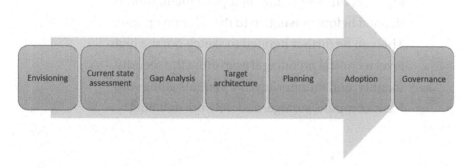

Figure 1-1. Cloud adoption cycle

1. **Envisioning:** High-level goals and objectives of digital transformation are defined at this phase. It is important to consider how an organization wants to adopt a public cloud and at what velocity, aligning it with the business requirements.

2. **Current state assessment:** Thorough assessment of current state architecture is important to baseline the maturity levels of an organization to adopt a public cloud. Based on the assessment, it will be easier to define the adoption approach, identify the gaps, and kick-start the planning activities.

3. **Gap analysis:** This exercise will help to identity that the application requirements match with the configurations available in cloud technologies. Any bottlenecks like legacy applications, hardware dependencies, platform mismatch, etc., should be identified at this phase.

4. **Target architecture:** The future state in the target public cloud platform, covering at minimum the logical components and their placement, should be defined before moving on to the adoption phase. This can be further iterated to sketch out the high-level technical architecture covering the security, identity, and monitoring components along with basic compute, storage, and network detailing.

5. **Planning:** The outputs from the previous phases
   should help develop a detailed migration/adoption
   plan. Risk mitigation based on the Gap analysis
   should also be factored into this plan. A dry run or
   POC can also be part of the planning phase to gain
   more confidence and iron out the challenges.

6. **Adoption:** The adoption or migration process
   should be done in such a manner as to avoid
   disruptions in day-to-day business. Sometimes
   it could be inevitable, but the impact can be
   minimized with diligent planning.

7. **Governance:** Post-adoption, many organizations
   find it difficult or overwhelming to adapt to the new
   technologies and processes. It is important to ensure
   that a governance plan is in place, which covers
   various factors like ramping up the organization's
   IT team, defining security cadence, as well as a
   monitoring framework.

Migrating or deploying a workload to the cloud is easy, but consuming,
maintaining, and adopting the new environment is the difficult part for
most organizations, especially when they have multiple clouds, several
autonomous organizational structures, and various toolsets on-premises.
Which one would work seamlessly and which one requires to be integrated
is a task that is most often-debated and discussed questions during the
build stage of any cloud adoption. In any scenario, however, there is a
learning curve that the IT services has to recognize and accept. Defining
new roles and responsibilities or establishing a CoE team that can help in
the process is important in this stage.

This discussion should have given you a fair idea of how cloud is
changing the way we operate, what are the key aspects any organization
look for when they think about cloud journey, key capabilities required

by the provider to support such requirements, how adopting a new tool or service requires investigation into its capability to serve multi-cloud deployments, and the learning curve to operationalize. How familiar the tool is, how easy to integrate and operate and what is already in use currently usually decides the adoption. We also looked at how Microsoft is committed to this journey and provides the assurance that their necessary tooling and support make this happen.

An Architect's Challenge

Traditionally, monitoring is an infrastructure or security architect's favorite subject and is discussed mostly at this level. However, with the challenges experienced early on in in the cloud world, it takes center stage during solution development, and the build and stabilization stage, ensuring there are no gaps when it comes to fully operationalize. Hence as an architect (Solution, Infra, Security, or software) overall, there are very common aspects at hand that require attention.

What is the current practice and who handles monitoring?
The lines are often blurred when it comes to monitoring different components of the application in the cloud. For example, the network team will focus on the network layer monitoring and security, the infrastructure team might look into the aspects of OS monitoring, while the application team will use application-specific tools to look out for application anomalies, performance metrics, etc.

What tool do they use, and is it compatible?
Most organizations will have existing investments in monitoring tools to monitor their on-premises datacenters. It is important to analyze the compatibility of existing tools with the cloud-based architecture, find a common ground, and reuse as much as possible.

Will the existing or new tool be able to monitor the existing workload on the cloud?
Cloud-based workloads are hosted and managed much differently than when they were hosted on-premises. Moving forward from IaaS, capability of monitoring PaaS- and SaaS-based services are also the demand of the hour. If this falls beyond the capability of existing tools, a new tool should be considered.

Will it be able to monitor the new application developed for the cloud?
Cloud-first development strategies results in applications with a sea of difference from their traditional counterparts. Also, it is often seen that organizations tend to move away from monolithic architectures, adopting a microservices approach in the cloud during modernization of their workloads. Monitoring tools should be evolved to cater to all these use cases.

What level of integration does it provide with on-premises tools?
Integration of cloud-based monitoring tools with on-premises tools is important to implement a "single pane of management" strategy. Hopping between tools is what any IT team would want to avoid at any cost.

What is the learning curve to adopt a new tool, and who provides it?
If the new tool being considered is drastically different from existing ones, the learning curve and time taken to adapt and well train the IT team adds to the timelines taken to completely operationalize the environment.

Can it provide end-to-end visibility of my IT deployment?
This reiterates the point of a single pane of management, where the monitoring tools should be able to give full visibility of the IT deployment health.

Will it be able to monitor my virtualized assets and devices deployed in the cloud?

Many devices like firewalls, IDS, IPS, load balancers, etc., will have their virtualized counterparts deployed in the cloud, either native or from third-party solution providers. The tool being used should be capable of monitoring the health of such a diverse portfolio of devices.

What about my PaaS and SaaS services?

With digital modernization, PaaS and SaaS services get introduced to the IT landscape, which will come under the purview of monitoring.

What data does it hold and where if it is a cloud-based service?

With monitoring data coming in from different sources, we need to ensure the safety of this data in transit and at rest as it contains valuable information about the current state of affairs in your IT landscape.

What is the reliability and scale of the system?

The tools being considered should be resilient, reliable, and designed with the capability to scale when required. As more and more applications get added to the portfolio, being restricted by the scale of a tool is not acceptable.

What are its analytics and telemetry capability?

Having raw data is not very useful, unless you can derive intelligence out of it. The tools being used should have the analytics and telemetry capability to get this done without the customer having to spend hours to build it in as an add-on.

Can it integrate with my existing ticketing and SIEM systems?
The goal of monitoring tools, in simple terms, is to bring any anomalies to the attention of the right people. Some tools might offer plug and play capability to your existing ticketing and SIEM systems, while some might offer it in parts.

How do I define my diagnostic and logging data storage?
Diagnostics data is often found to grow exponentially over a period of years, months, or even weeks depending on the scale of your application. The right sizing and management of diagnostics and logging data storage are crucial components of operationalization.

Are there any alternate tools that can do this in an easier way?
We need to objectively analyze the time taken for deployment and the learning curve as well as other factors like reliability and scalability before finalizing the monitoring tool.

Will I require a separate deployment for my monitoring system, or is it cloud based in its entirety?
If a new tool is being considered, it is smarter to consider cloud-based options as managing a different deployment for a monitoring system will introduce additional overhead costs.

What value does it provide in addition to my existing system?
If the new tool does not provide any compelling value addition, it might make more sense to integrate the cloud-based environment with the existing monitoring tools.

How much does it cost?

Some tough calls should be made whether to continue with the existing capital investment approach or move toward a pay-as-you-go pricing model.

What is the implementation and management overhead?

If a significant investment of time and money is required to implement and manage a new tool, it might be prudent to use a more cloud-aligned version of the existing tool with minimal configuration overhead.

Will it reduce my existing pain points?

Traditional monitoring tools may not have all the functionalities when compared to their new Gen counterparts, and these requirements should be evaluated carefully to understand the trade-offs. For example, you need mobile interfaces or applications to check the status of your deployment even when you are not in front of your computer, or it could be as basic as integration with your ticketing system.

Does it follow industry standards?

A matured monitoring tool is expected to support certain standards, say multiple probing and heard-bear mechanisms, out-of-box dashboards, reports, agentless monitoring wherever possible, etc. Any new tool in consideration should match up with these expectations.

Is it from the same provider or from a different vendor?

Organizations could leverage the existing support ecosystem if they transition to a cloud-based tool from the same service provider or vendor. Getting a new vendor onboarded and establishing rapport could again add on to the timeline of the operationalize phase.

Is it futuristic, and what is its future road map?
The capability of the service provider to stay ahead of the market requirements should be closely analyzed. How they have fared in the past and what is being announced in the road map are key factors in this.

Will it align with my existing security posture?
New tools should be able to maintain, if not improve, the overall security posture of your IT deployment. What more it brings to the table for the latter will be interesting to explore.

What level of automation can I achieve with this?
Be it onboarding, ad hoc configurations, or ongoing maintenance, automation should be built into the DNA of any monitoring tool. It is wasteful to spend man hours on items that can be easily automated using scripts or scheduled tasks. Maturity with respect to automation becomes one of the key decision points while selecting the monitoring tool.

This is new to me; how do I get best practices and recommendations?
Last but not least, the customer should get enough confidence from the vendor or service provider that an optimal monitoring system can be implemented in place using the tool, and the relevant best practices and recommendations required for the same will be provided. It could be through how-to-do documents, webinars, classroom trainings, etc.

Key Architectural Constructs and Operational Efficiency

We monitor for predictability, proactivity, security posture, incident response, and operational efficiency. However, it's important to understand how quickly you can gain insights from the piles of data collected in various forms, what reports we can generate to visualize, and how we can automate certain tasks to be more efficient and responsive.

Derive Intelligence from the Noise

The enterprise IT landscape is vast. Monitoring and logging information from different components often results in information overload. The monitoring toolset should have the capability to filter through this noise and find the information, trends, or occurrences that are relevant to the organization. For example,: a random event occurring intermittently in your server could point to a deeper issue that will go unnoticed if a proper trend analysis is not done. Manually writing queries to extract this information is cumbersome or near to impossible. Hence the tools should come equipped with these to quickly retrieve information relevant to your application's health.

Visualization and Reporting

As environments become complex with multiple component dependencies, it becomes difficult to pinpoint the root cause when something goes wrong. For example, a degraded performance of the application could be related to a faulty component in the hosting environment, faulty code, or even due to an organized attack on the front end. Getting results from querying the logs or checking the system health status of independent elements may not give you the big picture – hence the importance of visualization. When data from all these sources are visualized on a single dashboard with their dependencies marked out, it is easy to spot the stray element causing issues. Today, all leading tools come built in with some visualization elements or the ability to plug in to visualization services. It is the maturity of this aspect that should be considered in terms of ease of configuration, variety of reports, ability to interconnect elements, etc., while finalizing the tool.

Automation and Auto-Remediation

As explained in the previous section, the level of automation offered by the tool is a major deciding factor. In the event of an error, it is desirable that the tool can perform first aid through auto-remediation mechanisms. Using auto-remediation, you could nip many minor issues in the bud before it escalates, giving you breathing space for further root cause analysis. It could be a script executed natively by the tool or even an API call to another automation tool. For large-scale environments, this feature is a "must have" rather than a feel good add-on.

Incident Response and Triaging

Anything that goes beyond auto-remediation should be channeled to an incident response team. The majority of tools have alert mechanisms built in, where emails, SMS, etc., can be sent to relevant operations team members. However, this could lead to disjointed efforts with multiple people looking into the same issue when an alert is received. Hence the tool should have the intelligence to integrate the alerts with proper ITSM channels and triage it based on the criticality.

Summary

In this chapter, we looked at various industries and what aspects of the cloud interests them, as well as what capabilities they usually look for when it comes to monitoring. Non-negotiable capabilities, functionalities and features aligned to organizational strategy are probably some of the most difficult questions to answer. When we propose a monitoring solution, we should be well prepared to face these questions and how to address them. We should include monitoring as a main agenda item when developing or delivering a software, solution, or project. The monitoring tool or product is a solution on its own and should have all the important design constructs baked into it. It is an undisputed pillar for a reliable system. We cannot depend on our system's reliability if the monitoring system itself is not reliable.

In the next chapter, we will look into Azure monitoring and how it addresses all the various aspects we have discussed so far. We will also look at its core capabilities, and how to achieve them.

CHAPTER 2

The Scenarios and the Tools

The Microsoft Azure platform supports enterprise-grade, hyperscale applications providing all the economies of scale, availability, scalability, and security. This makes it a strategic and preferred choice for any organization to host their applications and workload. Every organization intends to utilize a single system that can provide end-to-end monitoring of applications hosted both on-premises and on Azure. Second, some organizations look to continue to utilize their existing Security Information and Event Management (SIEM) systems and integrate the Azure services logs. Now, let us look at the details of the Azure monitoring and diagnostic platform and how it integrates with the various systems and services.

Azure Monitoring Platform

Microsoft Azure provides a comprehensive monitoring platform and solution to monitor all infrastructure and platform resources. It helps by collecting, analyzing, monitoring, and reporting all logs and telemetry from various resources and helps to be more operationally effective, efficient, secured, and proactive. The Azure monitoring documentation contains a very beautiful representation of the service as an image here: https://docs.microsoft.com/en-us/azure/azure-monitor/overview.

© Bapi Chakraborty and Shijimol Ambi Karthikeyan 2019
B. Chakraborty and S. A. Karthikeyan, *Understanding Azure Monitoring*,
https://doi.org/10.1007/978-1-4842-5130-0_2

Basics

Logs

Azure produces extensive logging for every service. These logs are categorized as the following:

a. **Control/Management logs:** They give visibility into the Azure Resource Manager CREATE, UPDATE, and DELETE operations. These logs include Azure subscription-level and Tenant-level events and operations. For example, any create, deploy, delete resource operations, or any Azure Active Directory-level operational events.

b. **Data Plane logs:** These give visibility into the events raised when using an Azure resource. For example, these could be Windows Event logs from an Azure virtual machine; security and application logs in a virtual machine; application-specific performance and functionality data; or any other Azure resource-specific data, for example, Network Security Group logs or Application Gateway diagnostic data, etc.

We can enable these Logs either by PowerShell, using Azure Diagnostics SDK and Visual Studio; from the Azure Portal Diagnostics/monitoring settings; or by using a JSON template incorporating the diagnostics extension. The resource-specific logs can be enabled either at the time when we deploy the resource or anytime later.

You can also ingest data into the Azure Monitor from a custom resource using Data Collector APIs. This addresses any custom scenarios wherein the resources do not have an inherent way to expose any telemetry. More documentation can be found here: `https://docs.microsoft.com/en-us/azure/azure-monitor/platform/data-collector-api`.

Services and Resources

There are different services and resources that one can create on Azure. Hence, the collection methods and type of logs can be very different. Various Azure resources emit different logs; for example, VMs will have Event viewer logs and other performance metrics; the storage will have performance metrics and access logs, the Load Balancer and Network Security Group will emit other sets of logs. The collection method may be different in each case. We will discuss each type and its formats in our upcoming discussions.

Storing Logs

We can either store these logs in an Azure Storage account (tables, blobs) or Event Hubs, etc. It may be Event logs forwarded to a collector system. Hence, the logs, data generated by Azure resources can be XML, CSV, Evtx, TXT, or JASON based. We need to make sure to store them effectively and so that they are easily accessible and interpretable by the different SIEM system if required.

Exporting Logs

Azure has its own set of tools (Log Integrator) enabling these logs to be either streamed, exported into the SIEM system, or Convert them into a standard format, for example, JSON, which can be fed into the SIEM system. The preferred method is using a vendor-specific connector.

Monitoring Logs

The Azure Monitor Views and dashboards, Log analytics views, and PowerBI are all used to monitor logs.

Azure monitoring is undergoing several changes, including consolidation and integration of various separate services into it.

For example, Azure log analytics and Azure Application Insights were part of a separate brand called Azure Operations Management Suite (OMS), and they are now integrated into Azure Monitor. Although the data analytics are still being done by Log Analytics, Azure Monitor now provides the single pane of glass for a seamless experience on insight, visualize, and analyze.

Types of Data

Fundamentally there are two types of data that are in use in any monitoring system.

- **Logs:** Logs are a set of various data organized together to provide meaningful insights. It may contain additional properties or attributes: for example, Windows event logs that consist of various kinds of data related to an event. It contains time, user, details of the event, id that references the event and is well documented, etc. Then there are logs that might be specific to a service. For example, there are IIS logs, which contain service start, service stop, what is loaded, and what went wrong in the event of a failure of the service.

- **Metrics:** These are point-in-time information or numerical values about the system performance or other aspects of a service. For example, it could be CPU and Memory usage collected in a specific interval over a period of time. Depending on requirements, we can choose the sampling interval, and calculate and interpret values based on Max, Min, Avg, or Sum. Another interesting example would be Endpoints of an Azure Traffic Manager or Azure Application Gateway – number of endpoints available at any point in time.

Azure Monitor: First Look

To access Azure Monitor, you can use the "All Services" menu and search for "Monitor" once logged onto the Azure portal as shown in Figure 2-1 and Figure 2-2.

Figure 2-1. *Search for monitor in All services*

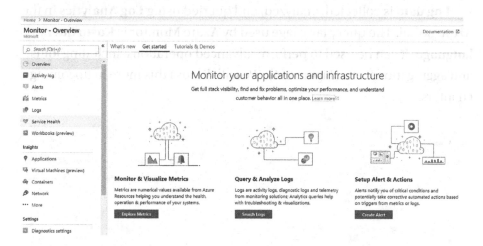

Figure 2-2. *Azure Monitor*

In the Overview pane, you have the option to create and review various charts using **metrics**, review logs, and create alerts as required. Here is a simple example how a CPU metric looks like for a virtual machine named CorpDc01. You can access and navigate to the same view from the virtual machine as well (Figure 2-3).

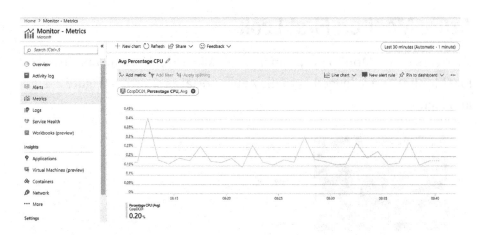

Figure 2-3. *Metrics explorer*

Log data is collected, analyzed, and queried using **Log Analytics** in the Azure portal. The query language used by Azure Monitor is **Kusto query language**. It can be used to perform advanced operations, including joins and aggregations, etc. (Figure 2-4). We will discuss this more in upcoming chapters.

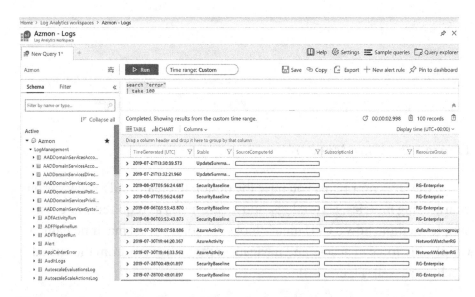

Figure 2-4. *Azure Log analytics in Azure Monitor*

Monitoring Data Life Cycle

Azure monitoring of a data life cycle can be explained with the help of Figure 2-5 wherein it goes through various phases, and specific activities can be performed to get better insight.

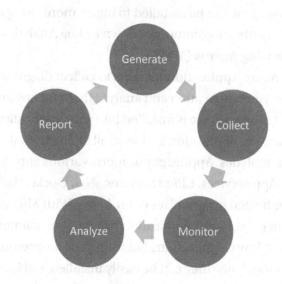

Figure 2-5. Monitoring Data Life Cycle

Generate

Azure Monitor starts collecting basic data from the moment a subscription is created or any resource is created in it. It collects all the subscription-related events relating to CREATE, DELETE, UPDATE operations. These subscription-level data are called **Activity Logs**.

Metrics of any specific resource is collected by the Azure platform once it is created. You can create various **dashboards** to review and analyze such data.

It is very useful for identifying resource performance and functionality issues and behaviors.

Should you require advanced, telemetric, and specific operational information, enabling **diagnostics** on the resources is the way to go. You can enable diagnostics for different Azure resources at the platform level and integrate those into Azure Monitor or other analysis tools.

For Compute resources such as virtual machines, virtual machine scale sets, a monitoring agent can be installed to ingest monitoring data into log analytics. These agents are commonly known as Log Analytics agents or **Microsoft Monitoring Agents (MMA).**

You can use Azure **Application Insights** to collect diagnostics information from your application and analyze them for any anomalies. A small instrumentation package is installed into your application to achieve this. It will monitor the application and send all telemetric information to Azure for further analytics. AppInsight supports various apps and platforms including Azure App services, Cloud Services, .Net, Docker, Java, JavaScript, Node.js; whether hosted on-premises or on Azure. With Microsoft Monitoring Agent (MMA) and Application Insights, you cannot only gain insights from your Azure applications but from your on-premises systems and applications too. Since they can be easily installed and integrated, you will be able to have a complete monitoring view of the estate.

Collect

Log analytics supports various sources to collect data Storage accounts, Event Hubs, Azure VM agents, and resources that can ingest data directly.

- Windows VM on-premises and on Azure: VMs with internet connectivity and with MMA agent installed, can report all configured logs to Azure log Analytics. However, in real life, there are scenarios wherein the systems do not have any internet connectivity, so a proxy service called Operations Management Suite Gateway (OMS Gateway) can be used. The OMS

Gateway works as a collector machine onto which all logs are collected and saved, and it is connected to the internet. The Gateway system is configured to connect and ingest data to the Log Analytics portal. A similar configuration can exist on Azure virtual network as well, where the outgoing internet connectivity is blocked by default by a network security group or a network virtual appliance firewall. OMS Gateway will help collect the traffic and ingest the log into Log Analytics. On an Azure VM, however, you can install the Agent as an extension that can be easily integrated to the log analytics portal that you specify. It also simplifies the upgrade process because since they are an extension, they are auto-upgraded without having to manually update them.

- Linux systems: Azure Log Analytics also provides for a Linux agent that can help collect System logs and performance counters from Linux systems. The scenarios for Windows VMs not connected to the internet apply here as well.

- Azure resources: There are a few different ways how Azure resources can ingest or integrate data into log analytics. These include the following:

  - Connectors

  - Custom scripts to collect and post the data

  - Integrated Azure diagnostic platform that can push the data into log analytics

  - Direct diagnostics data to a storage account

- System center integration: You can also integrate your existing System center environment with Configuration manager and Operations manager to extend your existing monitoring and logging functionality.

The Log analytics portal provides for these sources to be added as a source (Figure 2-6).

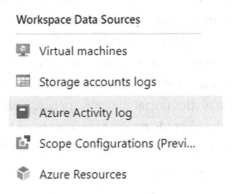

Workspace Data Sources

🖥 Virtual machines

⊞ Storage accounts logs

▤ Azure Activity log

⬚ Scope Configurations (Previ...

◈ Azure Resources

Figure 2-6. *Workspace Data Sources*

Monitor

Monitoring, analyzing, and reporting all are a continuous process. It all depends on one another and the continuous efforts to monitor the platform through metrics, alerts, events, and integration with ITSM systems. Fundamentals of monitoring remain the same even on Azure. A few aspects of monitoring include the following:

- What system do you wish to monitor?

- Why do you want to monitor?

- For how long?

- Are you troubleshooting an existing issue?

- Which metrics and in which interval do you want to monitor?

- Which tool and reporting system to use?

- What action to take if such events are important or requires attention?

- Who should be notified of such an event?

- How should he be notified?

- What actions are expected from that person/team?

- Is it required to open a support incident or log another event somewhere?

The overall objective of monitoring is to ensure that you are aware of the system's functioning or some important part of the system's performance and activity, and you want to achieve some level of SLA if something goes wrong with it. In other words, you wish to achieve Quality-of-Service (QoS). We will discuss some of these scenarios in greater detail in upcoming sections.

Analyze

Once we have the data from all various sources of your environment and collected in Log analytics, we can now query them to achieve our monitoring objectives.

The **Log Search** feature helps to query this huge amount of data, correlate them, gather meaningful insight, and take action on them.

- Create a simple Log Search query or an advanced query to filter or transform the data.

- Keep all your important repeatable queries saved.

- Identify if an action needs to be taken and trigger an operational runbook or an automation script to trigger another action, email, SMS someone, or create a service request.

Most IT organizations already have an IT Service Management system, for example, ServiceNow, Provance, or System Center Service Manager, and it is advised to integrate it with Log analytics. By doing so, service requests can be raised as part of an automation process and all necessary activities can be centrally managed and monitored. IT Service Management Connector has the capability for bidirectional integration to create incidents, alerts, and events in its ITSM solution.

There are also **Management solutions** that can be used along with Azure Monitor to gather better insights from the resources and services in use. You can either enable them using the Azure Monitor console or from the All services menu in the Azure portal. Once integrated, it can help to provide additional insight of a particular application or service. It provides built-in queries, and it views and leverages other Azure services to analyze data. Most solutions are not charged for its integration. They may, however, attract a cost due to the collection, usage, and storage of the data. There are solutions available from partners and customers other than Microsoft (Figure 2-7).

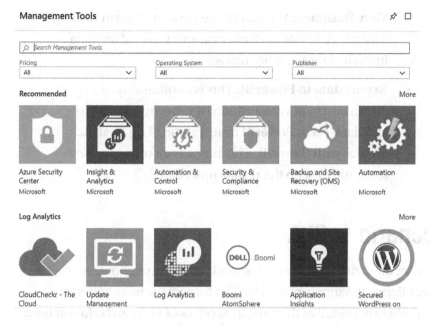

Figure 2-7. Management solution from Azure Marketplace

Report

There are various ways you can create reports and views to interpret the collected data. Here are some of the ways.

- **Log Analytics Dashboards:** This is the easiest way to create visualization for all saved searches that you may use every day based on your custom requirements.

- **Metrics Dashboards:** Similarly, you can create dashboards with all important metrics of your environment from different systems. You can include various views from various sources and create one integrated view. You can then publish them as a resource and apply Role-Based Access Control (RBAC) on them to ensure only necessary users can access them.

- **View Designer:** You can create custom views in the Log Analytics console to display various views of the data from the Log Analytics repository.

- **Export data to PowerBI:** This is another way to create beautiful visualization by exporting all results and datasets to PowerBI by integrating Log Analytics queries with PowerBI. The queries run on a specified schedule to keep the results up to date.

Scenario 1: SLA

SLAs are often defined in terms of availability, throughput, or response time. Microsoft Azure provides for SLA for most of its services. A comprehensive detail of the various services of SLA can be found here: `https://azure.microsoft.com/en-ca/support/legal/sla/`. Since partners and customers design, develop, and use their products and solutions based on the Azure cloud platform, they would like to ensure that the platform is able to handle the defined set of availability and performance standards. Hence, SLA monitoring is an important aspect of the overall monitoring solution.

Remember that performance monitoring and SLA monitoring are closely related. The primary purpose of performance monitoring ensures optimal system functionality where the contractual obligation to that defines the "optimal" state is defined by the SLA. It also defines what happens if the standards are not met.

Cloud solutions may include decoupled components, which means that multiple different services can be used to create an entire solution; for example, a simple web application can include three or more various cloud services; a virtual machine, cloud storage (blob, queues or table), SQL database. In this case, each service may have a different SLA and availability specifications. At the same time, designing such solutions may have included redundancy so that in the event of a single instance failure, the entire solution should not be impacted. Hence, while designing a monitoring solution, it is of the utmost important to ensure that all components of a solution is monitored to ensure the entire solution requirement is met.

SLA monitoring can be achieved by combining performance, availability, and health monitoring (we will discuss more on them in the next couple of pages). In our case of a web application, we should at least to the following:

- Monitor web endpoints on the VMs hosting the website;

- Virtual machine events and errors;

- Monitoring user requests tracing;

- Performance metrics of the virtual machine, storage, and SQL service;

- Service health for each system;

- Any other system's availability that is in use, for example, an application gateway.

You can also add diagnostics if you want to monitor what went wrong, when, and what time to identify and remediate granular levels of failure. Also, the overall system's uptime will not necessarily be the composite uptime of all services.

The SLA monitoring should result in identifying the overall aggregated performance values of the system, which may include:

- Percentage of time availability of the individual components during a period of time;

- Overall availability of the system as a percentage of uptime for any specific period;

- User response time breakup for each individual work item;

-. Overall user response time during a specified period;

- Calculate success and failure rates of the user requests during a period of time.

These Azure tools can help achieve create a solution to monitor SLAs:

- Log Analytics

- AppInsight

- Performance monitoring with metrics

- Alerts

- Azure diagnostics

- Azure service status

- Azure service health monitoring

- Azure activity logs monitoring

Scenario 2: Auditing and Compliance

Depending on the region, business, industry, or type of data an application handles, there may be specific legal or statutory regulations that require specific operations or all operations to be audited, monitored, and logged and saved over a period of time.

For example, banking or the insurance industry requires different auditing standards than an e-retail organization. Again, different parts of the whole system may require different kinds of data logging and retention.

Such audit data should be able to identify each user's action, sequence of events, time, and manner to ensure that appropriate authenticity and accountability can be determined. Since this data is very confidential and sensitive in nature, required auditing and compliance data should be stored and retained securely and only accessed by specific, responsible, delegated individuals. The assigned auditor or analyst should be able to generate various reports to ensure all legal, statutory, and compliance standards are met.

Microsoft Azure provides a list of tools and methods to meet any of these needs. Here are a few of the Azure tools:

- Azure Activity logs help to identify the various tenant- and subscription-level operations performed. For example: if a storage account was deleted it will be captured in the activity log with proper date and time stamp, the user who initiated the activity, which storage account etc. Hence, all series of events and details in Activity log becomes an authentic source of all subscription level and tenant level operations.

- You can maintain all activity logs as audit trails for a longer-term retention on Azure log analytics or on a storage account based on the organization's needs.

- Virtual machine system, security, and audit logs.

- Azure Active directory reports.

- Azure RBAC to ensure only authorized users have access to specific resources.

- Azure standard regulatory and compliance certifications.

- Azure compliance Manager (https://servicetrust. microsoft.com/ComplianceManager), which is a workflow based risk assessment tool.

- Azure Trust portal, which showcases all Azure data privacy, trust, compliance, and industry certifications.

Services trust portal is the one-stop location for all security-, compliance-, and privacy-related documentation; certifications, and audit reports (Figure 2-8).

Figure 2-8. *Service Trust Portal*

Scenario 3: Security

Security monitoring is one of the crucial operational activities of any enterprise today. All organization data based on data sensitivity or classification has to be securely handled, stored, and transferred at all times. The growing complexity of today's system also invites a growing need for data security, communication, and storage. For security monitoring, the key activities include the following:

- Detect any unauthenticated intrusion attempt;

- Identify unauthenticated and unauthorized data access and any attempt in this regard;

- Identify if any component or part of the system is under attack of any kind.

Most organizations today have already adopted a Security Information and Event Management (SIEM) system to include, analyze, and predict various events, alerts from different sources – systems, applications, devices, firewall, antivirus and intrusion-prevention systems. Apart from traditional security, modern organizations also explore ways to include new security systems that can perform vulnerability, port, and intrusion scanning in their IT infrastructure and deployments. This also includes cloud scale advanced analytics systems to aggregate, corelate, and identify security issues.

Azure provides a host of tools and services that can be leveraged to create a robust security system. It is not only secured at the platform level but also enables its customer to utilize the hosts of options to stay secure.

- With cloud, identity is the new security boundary with the diminishing border of network as a security perimeter. All logon events can be tracked and identified with Azure AD logging and reporting. Also, with dual factor authentication and location-based access and its reporting, this makes it possible to monitor global deployment scenarios with the cloud.

- All security, as well as diagnostic logs from virtual machines can be easily integrated into log analytics or SIEM systems to gain security insights.

- Role-based access control of each resource and implementing on-premises identity integration and monitoring really helps avoid the case of dual identity for the same user.

- Access-level telemetry of storage, network, and security center alerts can easily be leveraged to monitor any security issues.

- Azure has a host of other services that enable easy, scalable, robust monitoring of its resources and services.

Scenario 4: Availability

Availability monitoring is the cornerstone of the monitoring strategy of any organization. The simple truth is that if your applications and services are not available, you are out of business. Proactive monitoring and remediation of availability-related issues are high priority for any organization. The Azure Monitor service forms the nucleus of monitoring in Azure, acting as a centralized location to collate and analyze availability and performance information from sources in Azure as well as on-premises. Application Insights are the components of the Azure Monitor service that helps you track the availability of your applications irrespective of whether they are hosted in Azure PaaS services, VMs, containers, or on on-premise servers.

Application Insights

Application Insights, as the name indicates, is designed to give you deeper insights into the inner workings of your applications and flag any performance or availability issues. This is facilitated by deeper integration with the analytics platform that forms the core of Azure Monitor. It can be used to monitor applications developed in multiple platforms like .Net, Java, or Node.JS. It is also compatible with mobile apps, and can be used to monitor them by easy integration with the Visual Studio app center. Installation of a small instrumentation package in your application is all it takes to send telemetry information to the Application Insights service in Azure. Application Insights doesn't limit you to add the instrumentation package to applications hosted in Azure, which makes it a choice for enterprises with large-scale hybrid cloud or multi-cloud deployments. The response time metrics collected by Application Insights help you keep a tab on the status of application availability. The resultant telemetry data can be accessed and analyzed using PowerBi, used for configuring alerts, integrated to dashboards, etc.

A high-level workflow of how Application Insight collects and analyzes metrics from various sources is shown in Figure 2-9.

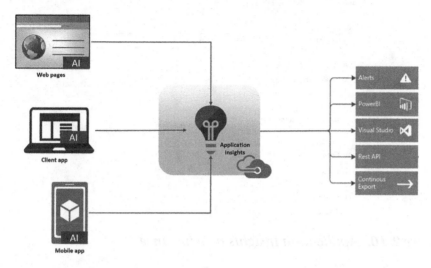

Figure 2-9. *Application Insights high-level architecture*

To start monitoring your application using Application Insights, deploy the service from the Azure portal. From the Azure portal, go to All services and search for Application Insights, select the service, and deploy a new instance (Figure 2-10).

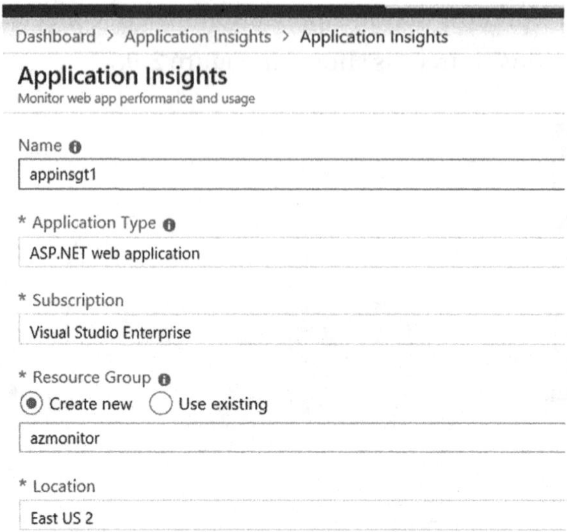

Dashboard > Application Insights > Application Insights

Application Insights
Monitor web app performance and usage

Name ❶

appinsgt1

* Application Type ❶

ASP.NET web application

* Subscription

Visual Studio Enterprise

* Resource Group ❶
◉ Create new   ○ Use existing

azmonitor

* Location

East US 2

Figure 2-10. *Application Insights new instance*

In addition to including the Application Insights instrumentation package, you can also monitor the availability of the application using the Azure Monitor availability testing feature. From the Application Insights dashboard, go to Availability ➤ Create test (Figure 2-11).

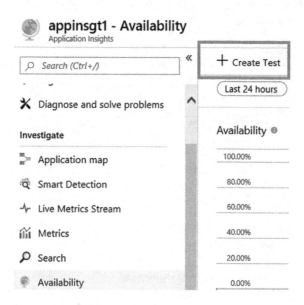

Figure 2-11. *Create a test*

Provide the required input parameters to create the test (Figure 2-12).

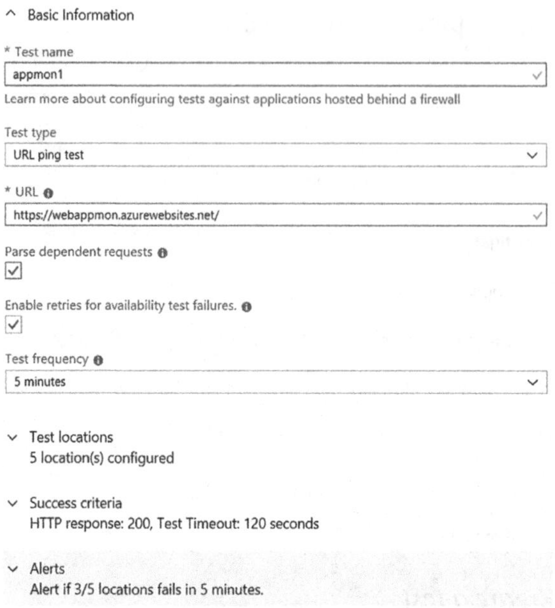

^ Basic Information

* Test name

| appmon1 | ✓ |

Learn more about configuring tests against applications hosted behind a firewall

Test type

| URL ping test | ✓ |

* URL ❶

| https://webappmon.azurewebsites.net/ | ✓ |

Parse dependent requests ❶
☑

Enable retries for availability test failures. ❶
☑

Test frequency ❶

| 5 minutes | ✓ |

∨ Test locations
    5 location(s) configured

∨ Success criteria
    HTTP response: 200, Test Timeout: 120 seconds

∨ Alerts
    Alert if 3/5 locations fails in 5 minutes.

Figure 2-12. *Inputs for creating a test*

Provide the following details to create the availability test:

- A name to identify the test.

- The test can be created for a single URL or a sequence of multiple URLs using Multi-step web test option. For the latter, the scenario should be recorded using Visual Studio and uploaded to Application Insights. In this example, we are using a single URL. Note that the URL should be accessible over the internet.

- Select the option of Parse dependent request to check the time taken for all the elements of the web page such as scripts and images to be available. If any of those components fail to download within the timeout period, the test fails.

- Enable retries to avoid false alarms raised due to transient issues. The test is reported three times within an interval of 20 seconds before raising an availability alert.

- Select the test frequency and test locations. It is recommended to have a minimum of 5 locations to isolate website and network issues. The maximum number of locations possible is 16.

- The success criteria in this example is selected as HTTP response 200, with a timeout period of 120 seconds. You can also configure the test to check for content match to check for a specific string (case sensitive) in the response.

- Alerts are sent when the failed location count is above the set threshold

Viewing the Insights

The availability can be reviewed as a line or scatter plot graph (Figure 2-13).

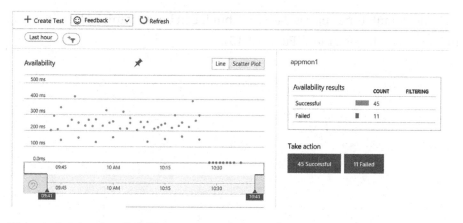

Figure 2-13. *Availability scatter plot graph*

You can also review the average availability of the application over a time span from the application dashboard. From the Application Insights overview tab, click on "Application Dashboard" (Figure 2-14).

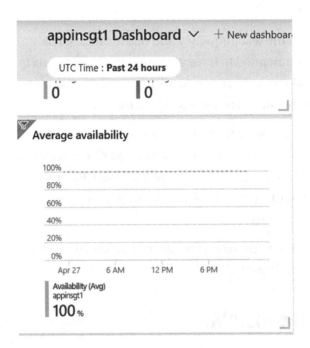

Figure 2-14. *Availability average availability*

The default time span is 24 hours, but it can be customized by clicking the filter icon in the graph (Figure 2-15).

Configure tile settings

Time settings

☑ Override the dashboard time settings at the tile level.   ▼

Timespan	Past 24 hours	∧
	Past 30 minutes	
Time granularity	Past hour	
Show time as	Past 4 hours	
	Past 12 hours	
	Past 24 hours	
	Past 48 hours	
	Past 3 days	
	Past 7 days	
	Past 30 days	
	Custom	

Figure 2-15. *Customize Time Span*

Scenario 5: Performance

Azure Monitor can collect data from various sources like applications,
VMs, or on-premises systems to give better insights to performance
of respective resources. Each source system needs its own specific
configuration as well as monitoring component service. For example,
Application performance can be monitored using Application Insights by
monitoring page views, load performance, response times, failure rates,
and performance counters of VMs hosting the application. For VMs hosted
in Azure, a set of performance metrics are collected by default by the
platform. You can enable Azure Monitor for VMs (in preview at the time
of writing this book) to get additional deeper insights on operating system
health as well as performance. If containers are part of your application
landscape in Azure, with Azure Kubernetes Service as hosting platform,
you can use Azure Monitor for containers to monitor the performance of
container workloads.

VM Performance Monitoring

Performance of a system depends on multiple parameters like response rates to user requests, processing time, volume of concurrent users, network bandwidth, etc. To ensure that the system is performing at an optimal level, multiple performance counters can be used on a case-by-case basis. CPU processing time, memory utilization, Disk I/O, Network I/O and errors are some of these counters.

To view the default performance metrics of Azure VM, go to Monitoring ➤ Metrics ➤ Add metric and select from available options in the drop-down (Figure 2-16). This example shows the Percentage CPU Utilization metrics of the selected Azure VM. Other metrics that you could select for performance monitoring include Disk read operations/sec, Network Out Total, Inbound flows, etc.

Figure 2-16. *Percentage CPU Utilization*

For more in-depth metrics on performance, health, and dependency mapping of VMs, you should onboard the machine to Azure Monitor for VMs. It is prebuilt with performance charts based on guest VM OS performance metrics. To enable Azure Monitor for VMs, navigate to VM settings ➤ Monitoring ➤ Insights (preview). Select the subscription and log analytics workspace to store the data and click Enable (Figure 2-17).

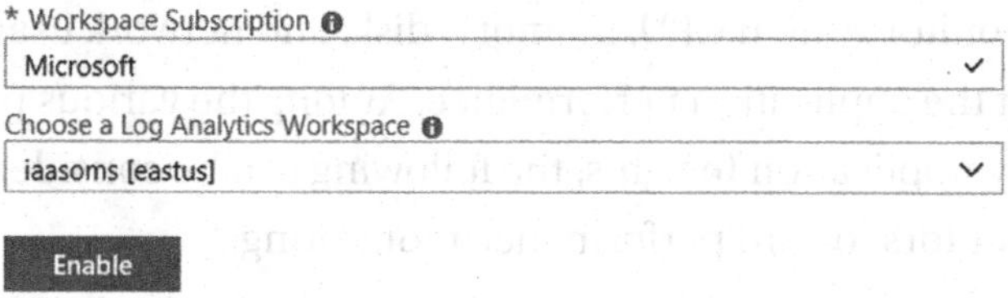

Figure 2-17. Select workspace

The Performance charts will be available in a dashboard about 20–30 minutes after the configuration (Figure 2-18).

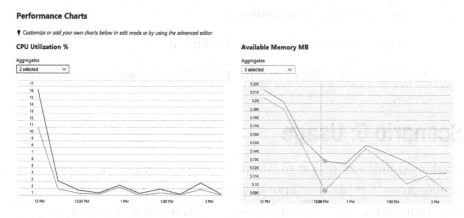

Figure 2-18. Performance Charts

Application Performance

Along with availability monitoring, Application Insights can be used for performance monitoring of your applications. Monitoring can be integrated using Application Insights instrumentation or even during runtime in the case of Azure Web Apps. If your applications are running in an IIS server on-premise, application insight performance counters can be used to monitor system CPU, memory, disk, and network usage that could impact the application performance. Among the various parameters monitored by Application Insights, the following can be considered as major contributors toward performance monitoring:

- Request times, Response times, and failure rates of application pages;

- The response rates of any external services that the application is dependent on;

- Browser or server exceptions;

- AJAX call rates, response, and failures if any;

- Windows or Linux machines performance counters.

Scenario 6: Usage

Tracking cloud resource usage is important for cost optimization and management, especially in large-scale deployments. Azure provides usage monitoring integrated into billing scopes, and the consolidated usage view is available from a cost analysis dashboard. Cost analysis shows the Azure resource usage and cost associated with it in selected scopes like subscription, resource groups, or even individual resources.

Cost analysis includes a feature to create a budget for a given scope and to monitor usage. This feature becomes very relevant in large-scale deployments where expenses could get out of hand if not monitored and managed properly. Permissions to create and manage a budget depends on the role assigned to the user. Users with owner permission for a subscription can create, modify, or delete budgets. Users with a contributor and cost management contributor role can modify budgets created by others but cannot delete them. They can, however, create, modify, or delete budgets independently. Reader role and cost management reader roles give users read access to budgets. You can also configure alerts to be sent out when a configuration threshold is met.

A sample budget is shown below that would alert stakeholders when usage exceeds an acceptable monthly threshold (Figure 2-19).

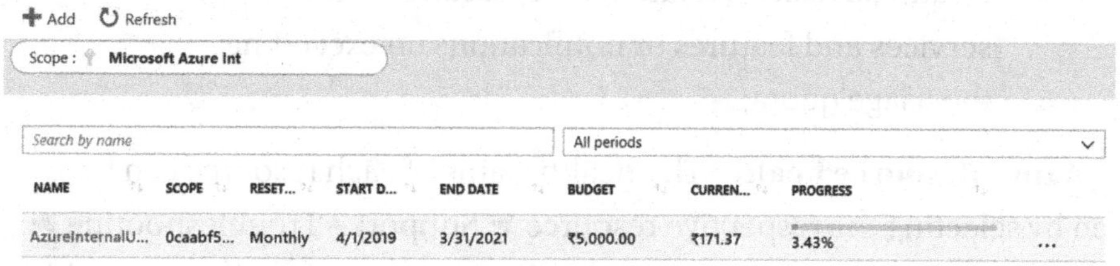

Figure 2-19. *Sample Monthly threshold*

Scenario 7: Health

While using Azure services, the context of health monitoring includes the health of the Azure platform, health monitoring of specific Azure services, and a level deeper into the diagnostics of individual resources.

Azure Service status page: Azure provides a comprehensive status of the platform in multiple geographies in the service status page that can be accessed at `https://azure.microsoft.com/en-us/status/`. The current status as well as status history is available for review from the above link. The status history shows previous outages, Root cause of the outage, Mitigation, and next steps.

Azure Service health dashboard: The Service health dashboard in Azure gives a personalized view of any Azure service outages as well as a summary of any potential impact to your resources. It can be used to create personalize dashboards as well as be configured to send alerts, should there be an outage impacting your services.

It covers the following three types of events that could affect the health of deployed services:

- Ongoing service issues impacting your deployed Azure services;

- Scheduled platform maintenance activities that could affect service availability;

- Health advisories related to deprecated Azure services and features or notifications on exceeding the usage quota;

Azure Resource health: The health status of each resource can be seen by selecting the respective resource ➤ Support + Troubleshooting ➤ Resource health. Any platform or non-platform-related issues that could impact the availability of the service will be notified here. Additionally, Workloads hosted in Azure VMs can have Azure Monitor for VMs enabled to give comprehensive component-level health data. This includes platform health, Guest VM health, component health, as well as the health of core services like DHCP, DNS, Firewall, etc. (Figure 2-20).

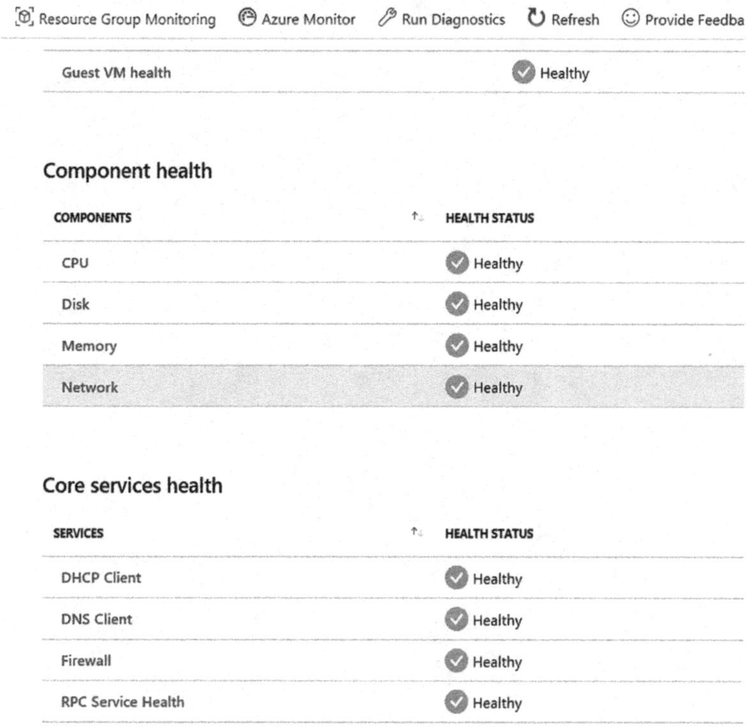

⬡ Resource Group Monitoring   🌐 Azure Monitor   🖋 Run Diagnostics   ↻ Refresh   ☺ Provide Feedba

Guest VM health	✅ Healthy

Component health

COMPONENTS ↑	HEALTH STATUS
CPU	✅ Healthy
Disk	✅ Healthy
Memory	✅ Healthy
Network	✅ Healthy

Core services health

SERVICES ↑	HEALTH STATUS
DHCP Client	✅ Healthy
DNS Client	✅ Healthy
Firewall	✅ Healthy
RPC Service Health	✅ Healthy

Figure 2-20. *Azure Resource Health*

CHAPTER 3

The Big Picture: Multi-Cloud and Hybrid Cloud

In this chapter, we will discuss and walk through a scenario at a broader level wherein an organization adopts a multi-cloud environment, integrates on-premises systems with the cloud, and deploys services leveraging Infrastructure-as-a-Service, Platform-as-a-Service, or Software-as-a-Service. This is a big picture scenario, and at some point, or another, any enterprise reaches this state to a greater extent. Monitoring at this stage may get very complicated and overwhelming, owing to the various tools, methods, and maturity level of the knowledge available. Figure 3-1 represents the scenario.

© Bapi Chakraborty and Shijimol Ambi Karthikeyan 2019
B. Chakraborty and S. A. Karthikeyan, *Understanding Azure Monitoring*,
https://doi.org/10.1007/978-1-4842-5130-0_3

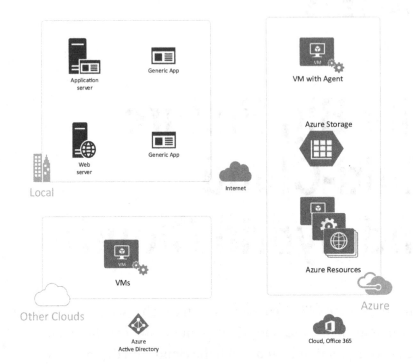

Figure 3-1. *Multi-cloud and hybrid scenario*

The Environment

There are different aspects of looking at the monitoring and ensuring all requirements are taken care. It can be based on Applications, the entire environment, or monitoring for a specific purpose such as troubleshooting an ongoing issue.

In our scenario, we have an enterprise with on-premises applications and resources. They have subscriptions from two different cloud vendors: Microsoft Azure and another leading cloud provider. Both cloud environments are integrated with on-premises and a good network connectivity exists with on-premises. There are applications hosted on Azure virtual machines and on Azure PaaS solutions such as Azure App service. On the other cloud service provider, the organization has a few virtual machines hosting some other workloads. There is dedicated VPN connectivity across the location/sites to ensure secure access to cloud and on-premises resources. They also have adopted a cloud integrated identity with on-premises, and all users use on-premises identity to access cloud resources. They have recently migrated to Office365 to replace their business productivity applications and use Exchange online; SharePoint online; and the Office suite part of O365 subscription, which is an end-to-end SaaS solution. To keep the overall scenario simple, let us consider this to be a single subscription, single tenant, and one-region scenario for the cloud environments. They currently have SCOM on-premises for monitoring their workloads.

We will not lay down any specific business, technical, functional, and nonfunctional requirements as of now. We will explore various monitoring options and services for our environment first, and then in our upcoming chapters we will try to achieve more.

Monitoring the Platform

In order to monitor the platform, let us first break it into components. Table 3-1 is a good start.

Table 3-1. *Platforms in Our Scenario*

Platform	description
Azure subscriptions	This is the primary platform that we wish to monitor as a whole. Subscription and regional services with respect to Azure Resource Manager and all required services for health can be monitored.
On-premises	The current on-premises system is also required to be monitored. The organization already has an existing monitoring solution leveraging the Microsoft System Center Operations Manager (SCOM).
Other Cloud platform	Any other cloud platform hosting various workloads. There might be additional efforts to integrate the other cloud platform and monitor them as a whole.
Azure tenant	Monitor the tenant-level services: for example, the Azure Active directory.

It is important to identify if we will require a single solution or multiple solutions to monitor all the platforms. In our scenario, we can just start with Azure Monitor. Note that it is possible that the other cloud provider may also have similar toolsets, and it is up to us to guide them which one may be most useful and best for them; and it is up to the customer to decide which one to go with. Now let us look at the tools that we can use (Table 3-2).

Table 3-2. *Monitoring the Platform – Tools*

Platform	Tools
Azure subscriptions	**Azure service status**: `https://azure.microsoft.com/en-ca/status/`. You can find all regional and non-regional services health, be aware of an ongoing issue at the Azure platform level or in your subscription. Also, look at any issue history here: `https://azure.microsoft.com/en-ca/status/history/`. **Activity Logs:** Also identify any subscription level to create, update, delete operations.
On-premises	**Existing solution:** The current on-premises system is also required to be monitored. The organization already has an existing monitoring solution leveraging Microsoft System Center Operations Manager (SCOM). **Integrate with Log Analytics:** We can integrate SCOM with log analytics and required logs can be either directly set to the log analytics workspace or collected at a management server, which in turn can send to log analytics. The latter is preferred if you want to avoid network traffic from all agents connecting over the internet to log analytics. See `https://docs.microsoft.com/en-us/azure/azure-monitor/platform/om-agents`. **Microsoft Monitoring Agent (MMA)only:** In a MMA only scenario, we can just install the MMA on the virtual machines, which will in turn report to the log analytics workspace. This can be useful for testing and temporary environments.

(continued)

Table 3-2. (*continued*)

Platform	Tools
Other Cloud platform	Any other cloud platform hosting various workloads. There might be additional efforts to integrate the other cloud platform and monitor them as a whole. Since there are virtual machines hosted on the other cloud, we can take a similar approach to monitor them as we did for on-premises.
Azure tenant	**Azure Active Directory Audit logs:** Monitor the tenant-level services, for example, Azure Active directory by integrating Azure AD audit and sign-in logs with Azure Monitor. You can also alternatively archive the logs to a storage account. If required for other integration, we can configure audit logs to stream to an Event Hub for sending them to non-Azure solution or to an on-premises SIEM system.

Health Monitoring

There are two types of health monitoring that we can address. Let's look at Table 3-3.

Table 3-3. *Monitoring the Services Health*

Monitor Target	Description
Azure Services health monitoring	It is possible that the Azure services are not responding over a period of time owing to an underlying platform issue or network issue. These are usually not under control of the customer and may cause widespread service or production outages if they are not known before necessary action can be taken to prevent this.
Agent health	The Operation manager agent or Log analytics agent (or MMA) may also become unresponsive due to an issue. It is advisable to know if any of the critical systems that are monitored have a healthy agent installed, reporting at specific intervals.

Microsoft Azure provides health service monitoring for both scenarios. Let us know understand those tools to take necessary steps (Table 3-4).

Table 3-4. *Monitoring the Services Health – Tools*

Monitor Target	Tools
Azure Services health monitoring	**Azure Service Health dashboard:** This dashboard can provide details of any ongoing issues, upcoming planned maintenance, or health advisories that may affect your current services deployed on Azure subscription. **Health Alerts:** It is also advisable to create health alerts for your critical systems to initiate automated and necessary action.
Agent health	**Agent health solution:** This management solution in Azure helps you monitor and identify the various agents deployed and reporting to Log analytics directly or through operations manager management groups. You can identify how many such agents are healthy, unresponsive, and not reporting data owing to an issue. This also helps you to identify how all your endpoints and scoped systems are geographically distributed and monitored.

Figure 3-2 is a quick look at what health service and health Alerts in Azure Monitor looks like.

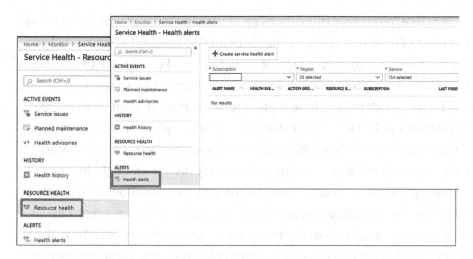

Figure 3-2. Resource health and Health alerts

Usage Monitoring

Usage monitoring should be able to help with items shown in Table 3-5.

Table 3-5. Usage Monitoring

Monitor Target	Description
Services usage	Which resources are used heavily and which are used in less volume? Which specific operations are in high usage over a specific duration?
User satisfaction	Identify user satisfaction level with varying degrees of system performance or usage.
Billing/cost	Identify applicable billing or cost. Enable Quotas in a multitenant system. Users are charged back based on usage.

Let us explore how these items can be addressed and with which tools. For most of the cases, usage is closely related to billing. To ensure that you are not over your spending limit, it is advisable to keep a track of the usages by resources and how much is spent over a period of time. Then you will be able to identify if there is any specific thread of usage in a specific department or in a specific environment. For example, in our scenario, if the organization is not migrating a lot of workload to Azure, it may not have any steep increase in Azure costs. It may just be a straight line too or just a growing trend depending on the new user addition or customer addition. The spending may see sudden increase if they are migrating their existing workloads to Azure or new projects are only been hosted on Azure. Similarly, if this is a Development environment, the spending may not be very high as compared to production; however, it may have sudden spikes in cost due to various development sprint cycles or test scenarios, etc. There can be other scenarios as well that may contradict the previous predictions. But, in all cases, it is a good idea to identify where the money is going.

Let us look at some of the tools to show us where (Table 3-6).

Table 3-6. *Usage Monitoring – Tools*

Monitor Target	Tools
Services usage	**Azure portal: Subscriptions cost analysis:** View a complete breakup of various services and over a specific period of time.

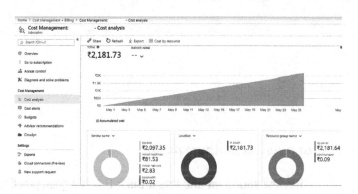

Figure 3-3. *Cost analysis in Azure portal*

	Resource Tags: Use resource tags based on environment, Organization structure, cost center, region, project code, etc., to identify and allocate cost of consumption.
User satisfaction	Use performance and availability monitoring to arrive at this value.
Billing/cost	**Azure Advisor:** You can turn on Azure Advisor recommendations to identify which are low-usage resources and on which ones you can save costs by turning them off or by optimization. Also, visit the Advisor recommendations page to understand the various standard recommendations to reduce costs (Figure 3-4): https://docs.microsoft.com/en-us/azure/advisor/advisor-cost-recommendations.

(continued)

Table 3-6. *(continued)*

Monitor Target	Tools

Figure 3-4. *Cost analysis in Azure portal*

Review your past and latest Bills: This is a good practice to review the bills, both past and current. to gain an understanding of where the pricing pattern changed.

Enable Spending Limit: Check your account portal of the subscription and see if you have a pending limit on. If you are using Credits, the spending limit will be turned on by default.

Cloudyn: Use Cloudyn service to enable necessary reporting and alerts that can auto-notify necessary stakeholders of various spending patterns and anomalies in spending. You can define budgets and threshold-based alerts.

Azure Pricing Calculator: It is also a good idea to get acquainted with the online Azure pricing calculator to estimate the monthly/yearly Azure consumption cost for various resources or before adding new Azure services. This will help gain better visibility to understand how you are charged or how much you will be charged.

Performance Monitoring

Performance monitoring is the key to ensure if the system is functioning optimally. We will discuss this in more detail in our upcoming chapters and explore how various metrics and values can make a difference in your design decision. For this scenario, we have various resources, so let us look at how and what we can monitor (Table 3-7).

Table 3-7. *Performance Monitoring*

Monitor Target	Description
Various components	In this scenario, we have Azure virtual machines, virtual machines on other cloud service providers, virtual network, VPN connectivity, VPN devices/gateways, Azure App services, storage services, on-premises systems, and applications. To be able to identify the performance bottlenecks, we need to monitor the key performance indicators for each one of them. Though we are looking at all possible components, it completely depends on the actual result you are looking for. For example, in our example, we may have SQL databases as well. We should monitor them too. However, these databases may only be used for storing some non-critical data and not used for any critical business purpowses. Hence, we may not be even interested in monitoring them. Similarly, we may just have two virtual machines, which run a very critical job once a week. In this case, we will be monitoring the systems during the time when the job is run.

Now let us look at our tool to monitor performance data in Table 3-8.

Table 3-8. *Performance Monitoring – Tools*

Monitor Target	Tools
Various components Azure virtual machines, virtual machines on other cloud service provider, virtual network, VPN connectivity, VPN devides/gateways, Azure App services, storage services, on-premises systems and applications)	**Metrics:** Every Azure resource emits specific logs and key indicators that can be logged into metrics to identify how it is performing or is there is an issue. Virtual Machine/physical machine (on-premises, Azure or on other cloud services): CPU Utilization, Memory utilization, Number of threads, Request queue length, Disk or network I/O rates and errors, Bytes written or read. Azure AppServices: CPU Percentage, Memory Percentage, Active Requests, Http 400x, Http 500x, Data In, Data Out, Average Response Time. Storage: (it also depends which storage services are being used, Blob, tables. or queues) Transactions, Ingress, Egress, Availability, Success Server Latency. Network: This is an interesting one. Since network is attached to almost all services, there are network specific counters for other services also that can be monitored. Again, not all counters will be monitored as a standard. Some of these may be monitored only to identify an issue or performance bottleneck, etc. VM - Network In, Network Out;

(continued)

Table 3-8. (*continued*)

Monitor Target	Tools
	Network Interfaces - Bytes Sent and Bytes received;
	Load balancer - Data Path Availability, Health Probe Status;
	Public IP address - Inbound packets DDoS, Inbound packets dropped DDoS, Inbound packets forwarded DDoS;
	Azure Firewall - Application rules hit count, Network rules hit count;
	Application Gateways - Throughput, Unhealthy Host Count, Healthy Host Count;
	Virtual Network Gateways - Gateway S2S Bandwidth, Tunnel Bandwidth.
	For a complete detailed list, you can visit the Microsoft metrics documentation site here: `https://docs.microsoft.com/en-us/ azure/azure-monitor/platform/ metrics-supported`.

There may be different counters for on-premises systems. They will, however, follow the same old practice of performance monitoring using metrics. Since in our case, we have SCOM, it can be easily used to monitor performance counters for on-premises systems. With the help of Azure Monitor integration with SCOM, we can now have better insight and analytics of the various performance counters.

Availability Monitoring

Availability monitoring and health monitoring are very closely related. Health monitoring helps to identify the current health state of the system, whereas availability monitoring is about the statistics of uptime for a system and its components. It includes granular identification of crucial individual component failures of a system. This is to avoid any future failure and take corrective action to maximize availability. Availability monitoring depends on lower-level factors and identifying the critical segments of the system that might cause overall availability issues. The recorded statistical value of all such components can be aggregated together to arrive at the availability of the system (Table 3-9).

Table 3-9. *Availability Monitoring*

Monitor Target	Description
Various components; All business systems and its dependencies	In this scenario, we have Azure virtual machines, virtual machines on other cloud service providers, virtual network, VPN connectivity, VPN devices/gateways, Azure App services, storage services, on-premises systems, and applications. For a better example, in our case, let's say the App Service depends on an App service plan and let's say an SQL database on Azure. There is an on-premises virtual machine that ingests data into the SQL database that the App service consumes to process the data and stores on a Blob service. If we consider this new specific scenario of the app service system, each dependent component is crucial to the success rate of the App service. Failure of either the Azure storage account, on-premises virtual machine, network connectivity, App service plan, Identity, or the authentication system can cause an availability issue of the App service. We may drill deeper to understand if on-premises VM accepts the data from some other system or who loads the primary data? An appropriate Azure SQL database plan ensures faster processing if required and/or no performance issues. Similarly, there can be several other factors as well impacting the overall availability of a system. Hence, it is critical to understand the overall landscape.

Now let us investigate what parameters we need to record to calculate such values and monitor a system's availability. Table 3-10 tries to explain some of the critical items.

Table 3-10. *Availability Monitoring - Tools*

Monitor Target	Tools
Various components; All business systems and its dependencies	**For all business systems and its dependencies -Performance monitoring with Metrics:** Required uptime and failures, timeouts, network connectivity failures, and connection retry attempts to be recorded. All data should be timestamped. All operational values to identify overall uptime and downtime of the system. Here is a standard formula to calculate the percentage availability of a service over a period of time by using the following formula: %Availability = ((Total Time − Total Downtime) / Total Time) $*$ 100 **Health monitoring:** For all dependent services. **Historical data** of same kind over a period of time for required validation and comparison. **Endpoint monitoring:** All API or web endpoints can be monitored to identify if it's responding. In certain scenarios, however, this may not apply. For example, even if the AppService/web service is up and running, its functionality may be in a failed state due to an internal server error or data corruption. You may not even identify this failure unless you perform some synthetic transactions or an error is logged in the system from the application side. Hence, only monitoring the infrastructure components or resources may not be enough. It may require additional or custom solution to be very sure that the system is available and responding to errors. **AppInsight:** It is possible to integrate AppInsight with the application to log all failures and errors or all 400x or 500x errors and trigger an alert to draw attention that something isn't right and the system's availability is impacted. **O365 Analytics:** Enable Office 365 monitoring analytics to validate.

Security Monitoring

One of the most important aspects of monitoring is Security Monitoring. Let us quickly look through the various aspects of security monitoring for our scenario (Table 3-11).

Table 3-11. *Security Monitoring – Tools*

Monitor Target	Description
Virtual machines/On-premises systems	All security, system, and necessary services event logs can be either forwarded or logged into Azure Monitor using MMA.
Storage services	Enable storage analytics to identify number of storage access successes or failures.
On-premises Monitoring	Since we already have SCOM implementation, all systems and applications can be monitored with security events and all data can be ingested into the Security Information and Event Management (SIEM) system for further analysis.
Azure Activity logs	Integrate Azure Activity logs into Azure Monitor through Log analytics to review any unauthorized access to the system. Accordingly, activity logs can be integrated with an on-premises SIEM system with a connector/plug-in for advanced security management and monitoring.
Identity and access management	In addition to on-premises Active directory monitoring and auditing, Azure active directory auditing and reports can be leveraged to identify unauthorized system access and attempts.
Role-based access control	Implement and monitor RBAC configurations regularly.
Integrate Azure Security Center Alerts with SIEM system	Azure Monitor provides the ability to stream the logs into Event Hubs, and SIEM vendors can write connectors to further integrate logs from the Event Hub into the SIEM.

(*continued*)

Table 3-11. *(continued)*

Monitor Target	Description
Network map	Use Network map to identify all possible network connections, configurations, and topology (Figure 3-5).

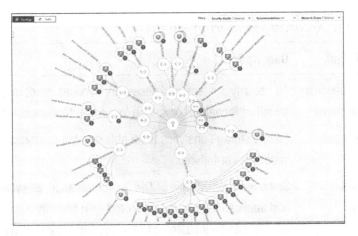

Figure 3-5. *Topology from Network Map*

Enable Security Center	Configure Azure Security Center and apply all best practices and recommendations (Figure 3-6).

Figure 3-6. *Security Center overview*

Auditing Compliance and SLA Monitoring

This part can be very specific to the requirement, and hence we would like you to review Chapter 2 – Scenario 1 and Scenario 2 for these two items.

Paint the Picture

At a very high level, the monitoring components for our scenario will look like Figure 3-7.

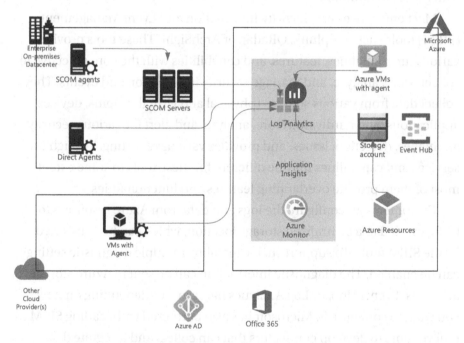

Figure 3-7.   *Monitoring components high-level view*

Hybrid Cloud Monitoring

In hybrid cloud architectures, it is important to ensure that the existing toolsets being used by organizations are put to best use while leveraging the capabilities offered by the cloud. An IT team shouldn't have to hop between tools to get a picture of the overall environment's health. Azure Monitor provides multiple integration points for such deployment scenarios so that you have a single repository for all your monitoring data. Let us explore some of the hybrid cloud monitoring options that work well with the Azure Monitor.

Most enterprises use Security Information and Event Management (SIEM) tools such as Splunk, QRadar, or ArchSight. These tools provide various functionalities, features, and capabilities with the core objective to collect, store, analyze. and manage security information and events. They collect data from various sources (physical and virtual systems, devices, applications, and hardware), store, analyze, and alert for various security anomalies, detection, issues, and provides various reporting. Though the services and capabilities may be different for these tools to some extent, most of them provide overlapping features and functionalities.

Customers can configure the logs and data from Azure resources to be forwarded to a centralized storage location, which can be consumed by the SIEM tools. To support such capability, multiple diagnostic settings can be enabled. The diagnostic information can be sent to Azure storage accounts, Events Hub, or Log Analytics namespaces depending on how you want to configure it. Microsoft has also partnered with leading SIEM tool vendors to develop connectors that can collect and integrate data from Azure Monitor. Azure Monitor integration with such tools can be achieved using different approaches. Some of these tools will now be briefly discussed.

Splunk

Azure Monitor Add-on for Splunk helps to collect and integrate data from Azure into the Splunk tool. The add-on at the time of writing this book supports Activity log, Diagnostics logs, and Metrics information to be collected and sent to Splunk. Activity logs are enabled via the log profile, and diagnostics logs as well as metrics should be enabled in the diagnostic settings of respective Azure resources.

The architecture uses Event Hub as a mediator, where the logs from different Azure sources are sent to the Event Hub initially. The logs will remain in the Event Hub based on the retention period configured waiting for it to be retrieved periodically by add-ons like Splunk. The add-on is configured to read information from an Event-Hub namespace, which could have multiple hubs, each storing different type of logs associated with a resource.

Steps to be completed at a high level on the Azure side for the integration are as follows:

1) Splunk uses the context of an AD application to retrieve data from Azure. This AD application should be created as Application type WebApp/API and assigned reader access to the subscription.

2) Create the Event Hub Namespace to which the activity logs, metrics, and diagnostic logs will be routed. It could be a single Namespace or multiple namespaces depending on how you want to integrate the add-on.

3) The Azure AD application keys and the Event Hub keys should be securely stored in a KeyVault.

4) Assign necessary permissions for the AD application to the Azure resources from which the data will be read.

5) Configure the Metrics, activity, and Diagnostics log settings so that the data is sent to Event Hub and can be pulled by the Splunk add-on.

A ready-to-use script is available in GitHub that will pull all required information from the Azure subscription required for configuring the Splunk plug-in. This script is available here: `https://github.com/microsoft/AzureMonitorAddonForSplunk`.

The script will generate all the required Azure configuration information that can be used as data inputs for the Add-on configuration from the Splunk UI.

IBM QRadar

To Integrate IBM QRadar, SIEM can be configured to collect data routed to Event Hubs using Microsoft Azure DSM and Microsoft Azure Event Hub Protocol. As with Splunk, the prerequisite configuration required on Azure side is that the logs should be routed to Event Hub.

The high-level configuration steps to be completed for QRadar to enable log collection are listed here:

1) Open port 443, 5671, and 5672 should be opened from the QRadar box.

2) Install the most recent versions of the following RPMs in QRadar:

```
DSMCommon RPM
Microsoft Azure DSM RPM
Protocol Common RPM
Microsoft Azure Event Hubs Protocol RPM
```

3) Once the protocols are installed, the "Microsoft
    Azure" log type will be available in QRadar along
    with the "Microsoft Azure Event Hubs" protocol
    when you try to configure the log source.

4) Add the Event Hubs connection string, consumer
    group, and the storage account connection string in
    the log sources configuration and deploy changes.

The logs from Azure portal will be available in QRadar on successful completion of the configuration. As per Azure DSM Specifications published by IBM, the following event types from Azure can be collected by QRadar through this integration: Network Security Group (NSG) Flow logs, NSG Logs, Authorization, Classic Compute, Classic Storage, Compute, Insights, KeyVault, SQL, Storage, Automation, Cache, CDN, Devices, Event Hub, HDInsight, Recovery Services, AppService, Batch, Bing Maps, Certificate Registration, Cognitive Services, Container Service, Content Moderator, Data Catalog, Data Factory, Data Lake Analytics, Data Lake Store, Domain Registration, Dynamics LCS, Features, Logic, Media, Notification Hubs, Search, Servicebus, Support, Web, Scheduler, Resources, Resource Health, Operation Insights, Market Place Ordering, API Management, AD Hybrid Health Service, Server Management.

ArcSight

There are multiple options available for integrating ArcSight with logs from Azure. One solution is to use the Azure Log integration service. This service should be installed on a machine that collects logs that will be sent to the SIEM system, in this case ArcSight. However, this tool is deprecated as customers are expected to use connectors like the ones provided by Splunk and IBM QRadar. The mart connector for Microsoft Event Hub is available in ArcSight SmartConnector 7.10.0. At the time of writing this book, the smart connector supports collection of diagnostics, audit, sign-in, and activity logs from Azure.

Multi-Cloud Monitoring

For customers with a multi-cloud land space, monitoring can be even more challenging as they would need to get a holistic view of resource health across multiple cloud platforms. As per Right scale's state-of-the-art cloud report for 2018, 84% of the organizations have a multi-cloud strategy. There are many factors to be considered while finalizing the monitoring strategy for a Multi-Cloud environment, and here are some pointers:

- Is it easier to use the native cloud monitoring solution offered by the cloud platform for each cloud?

- What is the trade-off when compared to the efforts involved in hopping between multiple tools?

- Can you plug in the cloud services to your existing monitoring tools? If yes, what are the advantages and limitations?

- What are the key monitoring metrics that are inevitable for your organization? Are they supported in the tools being considered?

- For adopting a new monitoring tool, what is the learning curve involved and the organization's investment toward the same?

Vendors like SolarWinds, OpsRamp, Grafana and New Relic offer multi-cloud monitoring capabilities to monitor resource deployed in cloud platforms like AWS, GCP, and Azure as well as on-premises environments. If you are already using monitoring tools, it is worth checking the availability of connectors to monitor cloud platforms using the same tool. Let us briefly explore few of these options.

System Center Operations Manager (SCOM)

System Center Operations Manager (SCOM) has an integration pack available for AWS to collect performance information from AWS resources and feed it into the tool. It leverages the Amazon Cloud watch metrics that appear as performance counters in SCOM. Alerts from cloud watch will be available as alerts in SCOM. The AWS management pack supports collection of metrics from AWS resources like EC2, EBS volumes, Load Balancers, EC2 Autoscaling groups, Availability zones, CloudWatch custom Metrics, etc. SCOM can also be integrated with Azure Monitor by installing the Azure log Analytics agent so that you have a single pane view of multiple environments.

Grafana

Another possible solution that can be explored in a multi-cloud scenario is Grafana. Grafana offers a seamless way of visualizing the data coming from multiple cloud platforms, thereby providing a dashboard view of your overall environment's health. Grafana has plug-ins available to collect data from stack driver, cloud watch, Oracle cloud infrastructure, Azure Monitor, etc., to generate insights. With Azure, the integration is as easy as adding a data source and providing an Azure AD service principal with a log Analytics reader role assigned to it. You can also integrate application insights with Grafana by calling application insights APIs with credentials that have permission to read the metrics.

Azure Log Analytics

While considering Native Azure monitoring solution, log analytics agents support data collection from multiple sources, be it virtual/physical machines on-premise as well as resources deployed in other cloud platforms. Azure log analytics is another solution that can be considered in both multi-cloud as well as hybrid cloud scenarios as it can pretty much integrate with any environment provided there is connectivity enabled to Azure Monitor. It also provides a single dashboard view of your resources deployed in multiple platforms, with built-in analytics capabilities to give you deeper insights and generate value from your monitoring of the data.

CHAPTER 4

Scenario-Based Examples: Cloud Only

In cloud first architectures, the monitoring perimeters are restricted to components in the cloud. The requirements for capacity, performance, and security monitoring can be met, to a large extent, using solutions available in Azure. The monitoring methodologies and parameters, however, could vary depending on the use cases or scenarios. Depending on whether the environment is greenfield or brownfield, the steps involved in designing the monitoring approach and implementation varies. Hence it is important to have a thorough planning exercise with applied due diligence before we set out to implement the identified solution.

This chapter will provide you a design and implementation reference guide for common cloud-only monitoring scenarios. We will also cover the configuration samples and templates for some of the use cases, including IaaS and PaaS components, which will help you with the implementations.

Design and Implantation Reference

Come of the common architectures for applications using cloud-only services in Azure can be broadly classified as shown in Table 4-1.

© Bapi Chakraborty and Shijimol Ambi Karthikeyan 2019
B. Chakraborty and S. A. Karthikeyan, *Understanding Azure Monitoring*,
https://doi.org/10.1007/978-1-4842-5130-0_4

Table 4-1. *Architectures in Our Scenario*

Architecture	Description
IaaS Only	These are "traditional" deployments in Azure, preferred by organizations adopting cloud for the first time. It is also used from on-premises environments that are migrated to cloud using a "Lift and Shift" approach. All application tiers would be front end, middle tier, and databases deployed and managed in VMs, providing customers more control over them.
PaaS Only	This approach is followed by "born in the cloud" organizations. It is also adopted when organizations can claim a certain maturity level in Azure. PaaS offerings, when used at different application tiers, enables customers to focus on the application rather than the nitty-gritty of infrastructure management.
IaaS and PaaS	This mix and match approach is commonly used when there is a need for balance between control and flexibility. IaaS services enable organizations to exercise end-to-end control on how they manage the services, while PaaS services offers the flexibility of outsourcing the management to the cloud platform where it deems fit.

Considering the popularity of microservices architecture, we should also add containers to the mix and the monitoring paradigm related to it. The choice of service for hosting containers could be Azure container instances, Kubernetes Services, and associated services like a Azure container registry. The monitoring strategy for a cloud-only environment is done over the following phases – Evaluation, Planning, and Implementation. Let us explore these phases in detail and activities to be covered in each of these phases.

For the ease of understanding the process, let us consider an environment that includes multiple PaaS and IaaS components to be monitored, for example, Virtual machines, webapps, App service environments, AKS, Azure SQl DB, Azure storage, application gateways, Azure load balancers, NSG, etc. We will go through each of these phases, covering the evaluation, design, and implementation processes.

Evaluation

The entry point of designing the monitoring strategy is taking stock of the existing environment in case of Brownfield deployments or evaluating the future state in case of Greenfield deployments. You can use the following pointers to develop a questionnaire for evaluating the environment and to identify the monitoring parameters. Note that the questions are not exhaustive, and you might have to collect more information at the evaluation phase depending on the application architecture.

What are the Azure components needed for monitoring of the application?
For this use case, we have identified the following components – Virtual machines, webapps, App service environment, AKS, Azure SQl DB, Azure storage, application gateway, Azure load balancer, and NSG.

How does the interdependency of components impact monitoring?
Identify dependency of the components being monitored so that false alarms or duplications can be eliminated. For example, a health probe-related error of a load balancer could be a duplicate of a VM health error.

Is it relevant to monitor network connectivity between components or to external endpoints?
When there are many moving parts and dependencies in the application, network connectivity monitoring between components becomes relevant. Network watcher offers extensive network monitoring capabilities using different built-in tools. During the evaluation phase, it is recommended to

identify the tools in the network monitor that can be leveraged to meet the interconnectivity monitoring needs. For example, if your application needs access to an external endpoint, the connection monitor tool can be used to monitor the latency to this endpoint over time.

What components are relevant for monitoring from a business system perspective?

There are multiple metrics available for each of the identified components. Enabling the right metrics and alerts are important to avoid information overload. For example, it makes more sense to monitor metrics of App Service Plans rather than App Service Environment metrics, as App Service plans have a 1:1 mapping to hosts allocated to them.

How do we identity the right metrics for the components?

Now that we have identified the right components to be monitored, the next step is to drill down and finalize the right metrics for monitoring. For example, if you are running a web application in VM with DB hosted in another VM or Azure PaaS services (mySQL, SQL, etc.), it is not relevant to monitor the disk i/o metrics. However, it could be the most important metrics to be monitored in a VM that hosts a database in an IaaS model.

What alerts should be generated and on what is the severity to be assigned?

The goal of monitoring is to flag any anomalies in the system and alert settings are the crucial last mile in this configuration. The specific alert settings such as condition type, threshold, sensitivity, etc., should be considered to assign the right severity to an alert rule.

What are the relevant actions to be taken in response to the generated alerts?

Azure action groups can be used to inform customers about a potential issue through email, SMS, etc. It can also be used to trigger remedial actions through automation runbooks called via webhooks or by invoking logic apps. It is in the evaluation phase that we identity the right course of action and identify the runbooks and logical apps to be created to execute it.

Planning

After the evaluation phase, the next step is to develop the implementation plan. This is not just a technical process but is closely tied to other organizational processes like change management as well. It is one level deeper than the evaluation process, where the parameters of monitoring are locked down and signed off by respective stakeholders. With respect to the different components in the use case, the monitoring configuration would be finalized during the planning phase. A sample outcome of this planning exercise is listed next.

Note: The planning outcome is dependent on the application architecture and the components to be monitored

Components	Monitoring Configuration
Virtual Machines	Performance metrics – CPU, Memory and Disk usage Disk I/O for SQL IaaS VM Guest OS Diagnostic data
App Service	Average response time Data in and Data out Http server errors CPU percentage Memory percentage
Azure SQI DB	Basic metrics Errors QueryStoreRuntimeStatistics QueryStoreWaitStatistics

(*continued*)

Components	Monitoring Configuration
Azure Storage	UsedCapacity
	ResponseType: AuthorizationError
	ResponseType: ServerBusyError
	ResponseType: ServerTimeoutError
Application Gateway	Metrics: Failed Requests
	Metrics: Throughput
	Metrics: Healthy Host Count
	Performance log monitoring
	Firewall log monitoring
Azure Loadbalancer	Data path availability
	Health probe status
NSG	NSG flow log in Network watcher
AKS	Health status
	Performance: Node CPU & Memory utilization
	Container performance monitoring through Azure
	Monitor for containers
Network Connection	Monitor connection to dependent component IP address
	through connection monitor of network watcher
Azure Traffic Manager	Queries by endpoint returned
	Endpoint status by EndPoint

Implementation

The outcome of the planning exercise is a detailed deployment plan for each of those identified monitoring components, which will be executed during the implementation phase. The following, additional pointers should be considered during the implementation phase for a smooth transition to operations.

How can the effectiveness of the implementation plan be tested before a rollout?

It is recommended to have a proof-of-concept period to test the settings and analyze the monitoring data for its effectiveness. This can be leveraged to fine-tune the configuration and lock down the final settings for implementation.

What roles and responsibilities should be assigned for managing the configurations?

For ongoing maintenance and updating of configurations, the right roles and responsibilities should be identified and assigned during the implementation phase. For example, while the ownership might largely remain with the IT team, application teams would need access to services like log analytics for troubleshooting purposes.

What role-based access control settings should be configured?

Once the roles and responsibilities are finalized, it would give a fair idea of the RBAC permissions to be configured. Any custom roles to be used should also be implemented during this phase

What services and configurations should be used for auto-remediation?

Options like runbooks and logic apps are available to be incorporated with alerts for auto-remediating issues. These runbooks and logic apps will be developed, tested, and deployed during the implementation phase.

What are the plans for operations training and handover?

The operations team should be given adequate training and documentation so that they can take over the monitoring of the components in the cloud. This effort required in the handover depends to a great extent on the expertise of the operations team in handling cloud monitoring.

In the next section we will cover the implementation details more closely for a few sample use cases.

Monitoring a Simple WebApplication on Azure

Let us consider the following use case of a three-tier web application with the sample architecture given in Figure 4-1.

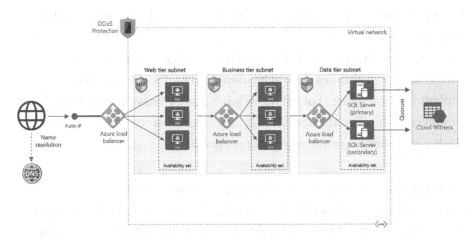

Figure 4-1. *Sample three-tier application*

As established in the planning section, monitoring will be configured for the following components.

Components	Monitoring Configuration
Virtual Machines	Performance metrics – CPU, Memory and Disk usage
	Disk I/O for SQL IaaS VM
	Guest OS Diagnostic data
Azure Loadbalancer	Data path availability
	Health probe status
	Load balancer health status

Components	Monitoring Configuration
NSG	NSG flow log in Network watcher
Network connection	Monitor connection to dependent component IP address through connection monitor of network watcher

Virtual Machines

The parameters to be monitored here are CPU, memory, and disk usage.

CPU Monitoring

CPU monitoring is available through the basic metrics of a VM without any additional configuration. This information can be accessed from VM settings ➤ Monitoring ➤ Metrics (Figure 4-2).

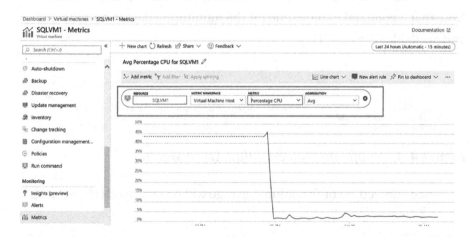

Figure 4-2. *VM metrics*

Memory Percentage

To get memory usage details, you will have to enable VM insights from VM Settings ➤ Monitoring ➤ Insights (preview). Provide the workspace subscription and name and click enabled (Figure 4-3).

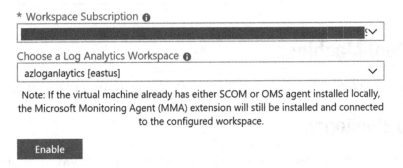

Figure 4-3. *Workspace details*

Once enabled, you see a notification that insights is being enabled. Note that it could take some time for the monitoring data to be collected and available (Figure 4-4).

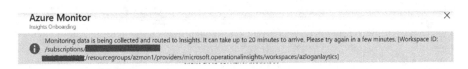

Figure 4-4. *Notification on enabling Azure Monitor*

Once enabled, a confirmation message will be displayed (Figure 4-5).

Figure 4-5. *Confirmation message*

From the VM insights dashboard, you can now view the Available memory usage and also pin the chart to the Dashboard (Figure 4-6).

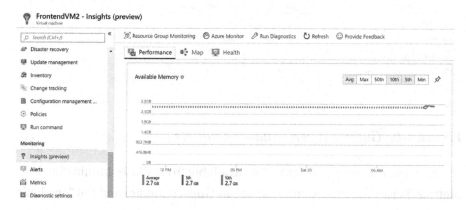

Figure 4-6. *Available memory*

You can also collect the memory usage metrics by enabling the guest OS diagnostics. To enable Guest-level monitoring, browse to VM ➤ Diagnostic settings ➤ "Enable guest-level monitoring" (Figure 4-7).

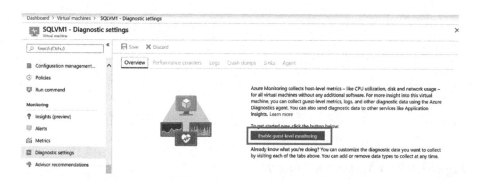

Figure 4-7. *Enable guest-level monitoring*

By default, the guest VM performance counters for CPU, Memory, Disk, and Network will be enabled (Figure 4-8).

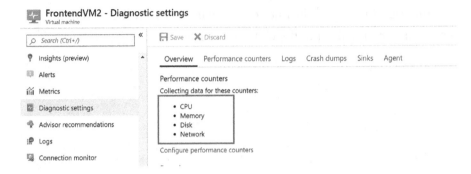

Figure 4-8. *Guest VM performance counters*

Now the memory metrics will be available from VM ➤ monitoring ➤ Metrics. Select the metrics namespace as Guest (Classic) and the "Available Bytes" memory counter (Figure 4-9).

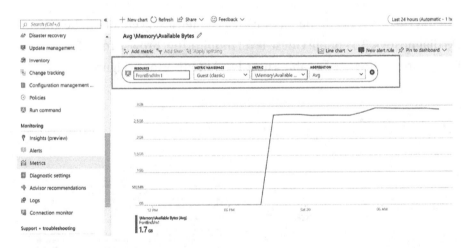

Figure 4-9. *VM memory metrics*

Disk Monitoring

To monitor free disk space in a VM, the "%Free space" counter can be used (Figure 4-10).

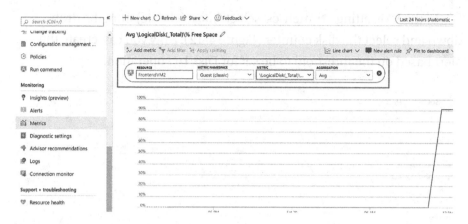

Figure 4-10. *Free disk space metrics*

You can fine-tune the settings if you click on "Configure performance counters" from monitoring ➤ Diagnostics settings of the VM and select only the required counters. For example, for SQL VM in the architecture, you need only Disk I/O-related counters. From the diagnostics settings, click on the performance counters tab. Click on the Custom switch and select the disk i/o related counters and click save (Figure 4-11).

Search (Ctrl+/)	Save Discard		
Auto-shutdown	None Basic **Custom**		
Backup	Configure the performance counters to collect, and how often they should be sampled:		
Disaster recovery			Add
Update management	**PERFORMANCE COUNTER**	**SAMPLE RATE (SECONDS)**	**UNIT**
Inventory	☐ \LogicalDisk(_Total)\% Disk Time	60	Percent
Change tracking	☐ \LogicalDisk(_Total)\% Disk Read Time	60	Percent
Configuration management...	☐ \LogicalDisk(_Total)\% Disk Write Time	60	Percent
Policies	☐ \LogicalDisk(_Total)\% Idle Time	60	Percent
Run command	☐ \LogicalDisk(_Total)\Disk Bytes/sec	60	BytesPerSecond
Monitoring	☐ \LogicalDisk(_Total)\Disk Read Bytes/sec	60	BytesPerSecond
Insights (preview)	☐ \LogicalDisk(_Total)\Disk Write Bytes/sec	60	BytesPerSecond
Alerts	☑ \LogicalDisk(_Total)\Disk Transfers/sec	60	BytesPerSecond
Metrics	☑ \LogicalDisk(_Total)\Disk Reads/sec	60	BytesPerSecond
Diagnostic settings	☑ \LogicalDisk(_Total)\Disk Writes/sec	60	BytesPerSecond

Figure 4-11. *Custom Switch configuration*

In the VM settings ➤ metrics, select Guest (classic) from the drop-down and select the disk counter (Figure 4-12). Now you can create the alert based on the threshold to be set for Disk I/O operation.

Figure 4-12. Disk counter Metrics

Azure Load Balancer

Monitoring configurations are slightly different for basic and standard load balancers. For basic load balancers, the settings are to be enabled from load balancer ➤ Configure monitoring ➤ Diagnostic settings ➤ Add Diagnostic settings.

In the Diagnostic settings, select the storage account, Event Hub, or log analytics workspace where the diagnostics data should be forwarded to. Since data from all components are being sent to log analytics, the same workspace is selected in this example. The diagnostics data for the load balancer will now be available in Log Analytics for review (Figure 4-13).

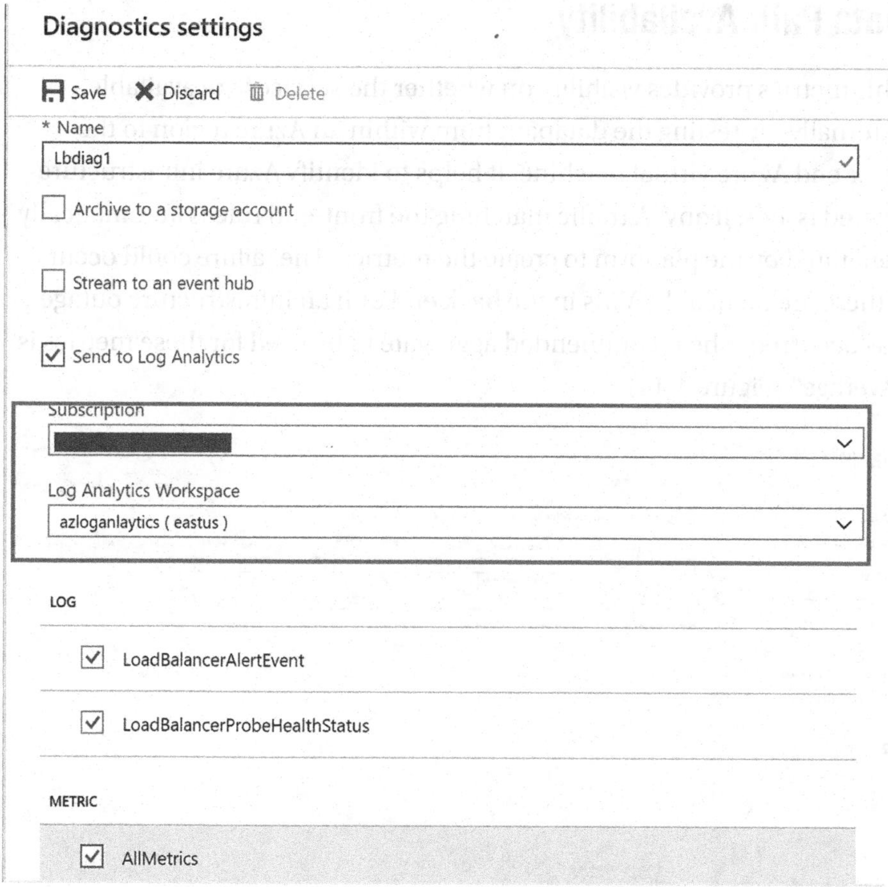

Diagnostics settings

💾 Save   ✖ Discard   🗑 Delete

* Name

| Lbdiag1 | ✓ |

☐ Archive to a storage account

☐ Stream to an event hub

☑ Send to Log Analytics

Subscription

| ▓▓▓▓▓▓▓ | ∨ |

Log Analytics Workspace

| azloganlaytics (eastus) | ∨ |

LOG

☑ LoadBalancerAlertEvent

☑ LoadBalancerProbeHealthStatus

METRIC

☑ AllMetrics

Figure 4-13. *Load balancer diagnostics configuration*

A standard load balancer is the recommended one for all new deployments as it supports features like availability zones, HA ports, HTTPS health probes, as well as the flexibility to add a combination of virtual machines, availability sets, and VMSS in the back-end pools. With respect to diagnostics, standard load balancers support multidimensional metrics for health probe status, byte, and packet counters, outbound connection health, etc.

Data Path Availability

This metrics provides visibility on whether the services are available externally, by testing the datapath from within an Azure region to the back-end Azure virtual machine. It helps to identify Azure infrastructure-related issues, if any. A traffic matching the front-end rule is automatically generated by the platform to create the metrics. The failure could occur if there are no healthy VMs in the back end or if an infrastructure outage has occurred. The recommended aggregate to be used for these metrics is "Average" (Figure 4-14).

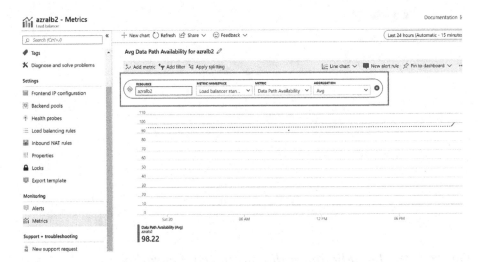

Figure 4-14. *Data path availability Metrics*

You can also select apply Splitting and choose the Frontend IP address or Frontend port as an additional dimension for monitoring (Figure 4-15)

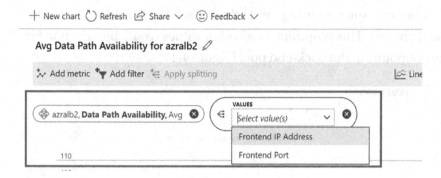

Figure 4-15. *Data path availability Metrics Values*

Health Probe Status

This metrics gives an overview of the health probe of the application, based on the instance endpoints configured. This metrics will show downtime if the service is unavailable or if there is any configuration like NSG or firewall blocking access to the endpoints (Figure 4-16).

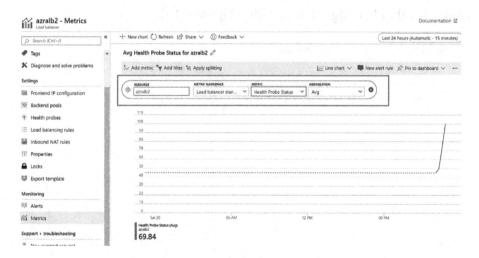

Figure 4-16. *Health probe status Metrics*

Click on "Apply splitting" and select "Backend IP Address" from the listed options. This is optimal as all other values would be the same for all the endpoints in the back-end pool (Figure 4-17).

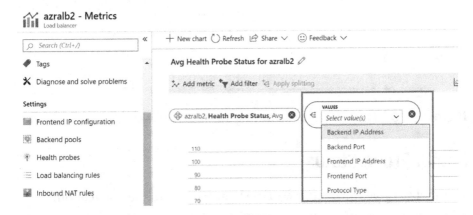

Figure 4-17. *Health probe status Metrics values*

As can be seen in the next example, one of the endpoints was down, while the other had higher availability (Figure 4-18).

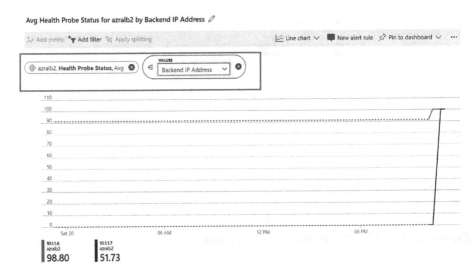

Figure 4-18. *Backend IP address status*

NSG

For monitoring NSG flow, Azure Network watcher should be enabled
for the region. Search for network watcher from all services in the Azure
portal. In the overview tab, expand regions and make sure that service is
enabled in the target region where the NSG is created. The next step is to
enable the NSG flow logs.

From Network watcher ➤ Logs ➤ NSG flow logs, filter down to the
NSGs where the flow logs need to be enabled. Click on the NSG to open
the flow log settings.

Select from between Version 1 and Version 2. Version 1 provides
ingress and egress traffic information for packets that have been allowed
and denied. Version 2 provides additional information on the flow state
starting from when the flow is initiated to continuation and termination of
the flow along with the traffic bandwidth details.

Also, select the storage accounts to which the flow logs will be stored.
The raw data can be downloaded from the storage account, or it can be
analyzed using a traffic analytics solution (Figure 4-19).

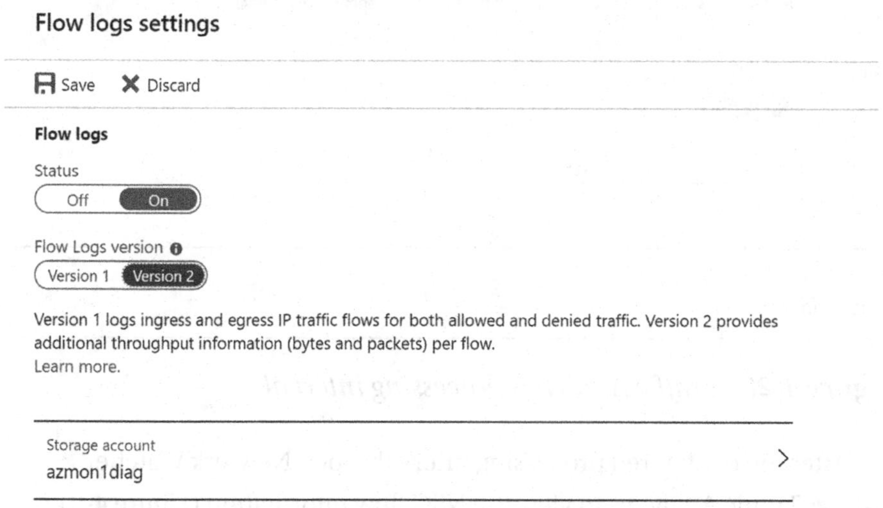

Flow logs settings

💾 Save   ✖ Discard

Flow logs

Status

(Off   ▐ On ▌)

Flow Logs version ❶

(Version 1 ▐ Version 2 ▌)

Version 1 logs ingress and egress IP traffic flows for both allowed and denied traffic. Version 2 provides
additional throughput information (bytes and packets) per flow.
Learn more.

Storage account
azmon1diag   >

Figure 4-19. *Flow log settings*

In the same window you can configure the number of days for which the logs will be stored. You can also enable Traffic analytics to visualize the network activity by leveraging the NSG flow logs. It also helps to identify the traffic flow patterns within Azure and also from the internet, giving valuable insights to optimize performance and capacity.

Note that this configuration needs a log analytics workspace where a network performance monitor solution will be installed. The processing interval can be configured to be either 10 minutes or 1 hour (Figure 4-20).

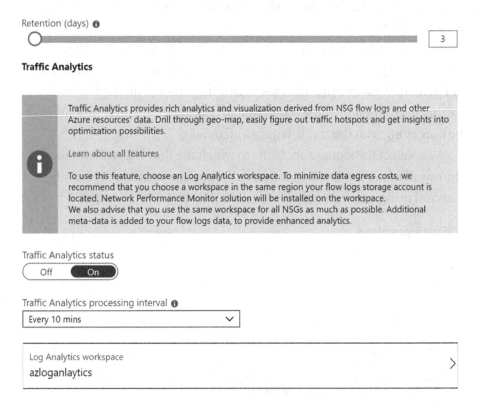

Figure 4-20. *Traffic Analytics processing interval*

After the configured processing interval, Open Network Watcher ➤ Logs ➤ Traffic Analytics to view the NSG flow information (Figure 4-21).

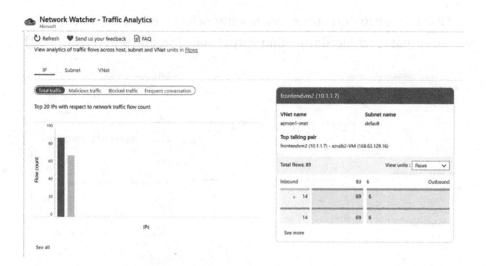

Figure 4-21. *NSG Flow information*

You can drill down to additional details such as Malicious traffic, Blocked traffic, or Frequent conversation from the collected NSG flow information at IP/Subnet/VNet level.

Network Connection

The connection watcher service of network watcher enables connectivity monitoring from a virtual machine to another VM, FQDN, URI, or IP address. This is helpful in monitoring dependent application components and to identify if the network traffic is getting blocked. The connection monitor is also capable of providing potential reasons for a connectivity issue such as DNS resolution issue, custom route-related issue, VM security rules, etc. The data is available over a period of time in terms of minimum, maximum, and average latency observed between the VM and the endpoint.

To monitor a network connection using a connection watcher, browse to network watcher ➤ Monitoring ➤ Connection monitor and Click on +Add.

Give a name to the connection monitor, select the source subscription, source virtual machine, destination virtual machine, and port (Figure 4-22).

Figure 4-22. *Connection monitor configuration*

If you click on the connection monitor, the details pane will be displayed on the bottom pane. You can click to view the graph in a new window (Figure 4-23).

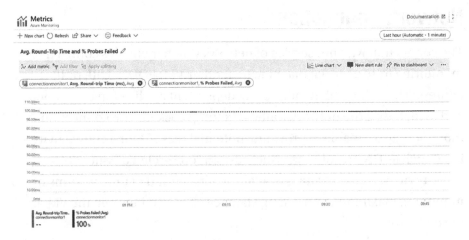

Figure 4-23. *Connection monitor graph*

You can also see the grid view and topology view from the connection monitor (Figure 4-24).

Grid view   Topology view

Hops

NAME	IP ADDRESS	STATUS	NEXT HOP IP ADDRESS	RTT FROM SOURCE (MS)
🖥 Businesstier0	10.0.0.5	ⓘ	10.1.1.5	-
🖥 SQLVM1	10.1.1.5	✅	-	-

Grid view   **Topology view**

Businesstier0   SQLVM1
10.0.0.5   10.1.1.5

Figure 4-24.   Connection monitor grid view

Monitoring Application That Includes PaaS and IaaS Services

Let us consider the sample architecture of a two-tier web application that uses webapp in the front end, connecting to SQL VMs in the back end (Figure 4-25).

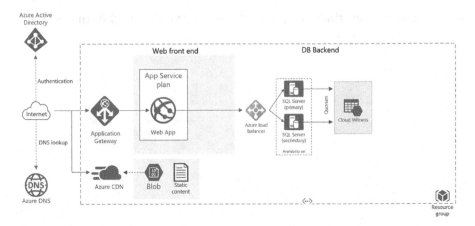

Figure 4-25. *Sample two-tier application*

As established in the planning section, monitoring will be configured for the following components.

Components	Monitoring Configuration
App service environment	Average response time
	Data in and Data out
	Http server errors
	CPU percentage
	Memory percentage
Azure Storage	UsedCapacity
	ResponseType: AuthorizationError
	ResponseType: ServerBusyError
	ResponseType: ServerTimeoutError
Application Gateway	Metrics: Failed Requests
	Metrics: Throughput
	Metrics: Healthy Host Count
	Performance log monitoring
	Firewall log monitoring

Azure Storage

UsedCapacity: Azure storage capacity metrics can be leveraged here to monitor the used capacity. While using standard storage, the value is the sum of capacity consumed by all tables, blobs, and queues in the storage. For premium storage and blob storage, values will be equivalent to the capacity used by all blobs in the storage.

In this example, we are using standard storage. From the Storage setting ➤ Monitoring ➤ Metrics, select metrics "Used Capacity" listed in the drop-down under Capacity (Figure 4-26).

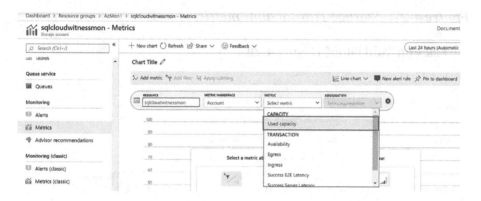

Figure 4-26. *Storage metrics selection*

ResponseType:"Authorization error" helps to track any unauthorized access of data in the storage account and is important to monitor from a data security perspective. To monitor the ResponseType, select the metrics type as Transactions (Figure 4-27).

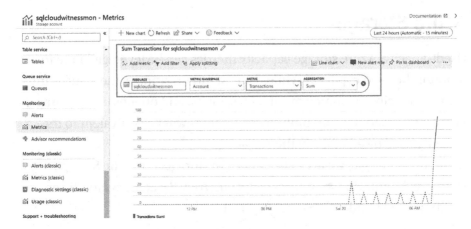

Figure 4-27. *Storage Transactions metrics*

Click on "Add Filter" (Figure 4-28).

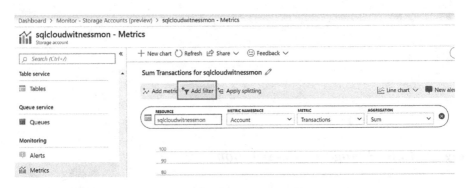

Figure 4-28. *Storage Transactions metrics filter*

Select Property as ResponseType and value as "AuthorizationError" (Figure 4-29).

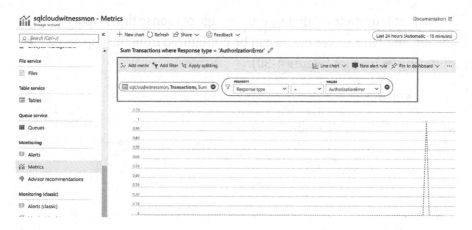

Figure 4-29. "AuthorizationError" filter

App Service

The identified metrics for App Service are the following:

- Average response time: It is the time taken in milliseconds by the app to respond to serve requests.

- Data in and Data out: Monitors the data in and out of the bandwidth consumed by the application in MiB.

- Http server errors: Count of requests that result in an Http status code greater than or equal to 500 but less than 600.

- CPU percentage: This metric will be used at the app service plan level to monitor the CPU usage across all instances of the plan.

- Memory percentage: This metric is also used for the app service plan, to monitor the memory usage across all instances.

107

The first four metrics, that is, the Average response time, Data in, Data out, and Http server errors can be configured from the app service ➤ monitoring ➤ metrics (Figure 4-30).

Figure 4-30. *App Service metrics*

For CPU and memory percentage monitoring for all instances, browse to app service plan ➤ Monitoring ➤ Metrics and select the metrics (Figure 4-31).

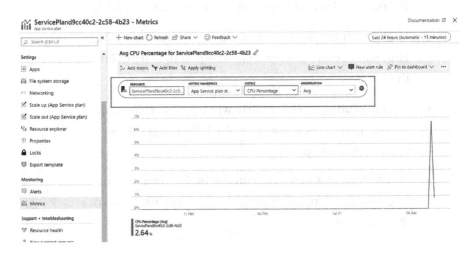

Figure 4-31. *CPU Percentage metrics*

Application Gateway

Both metrics and log files should be monitored for an application gateway. The metrics can be monitored the same way as in other components, that is, from Application gateway ➤ Monitoring ➤ Metrics (Figure 4-32).

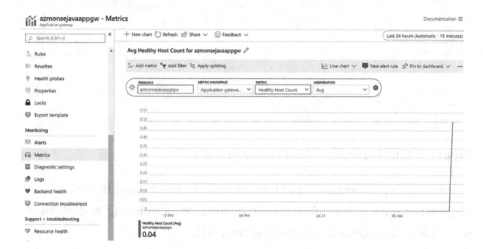

Figure 4-32. *Healthy host count metrics*

The healthy host count and unhealthy host count information can be further drilled down to a specific back-end pool. This is useful when the application gateway is used for multiple applications and you want to monitor the status of one specific application back-end pool (Figure 4-33).

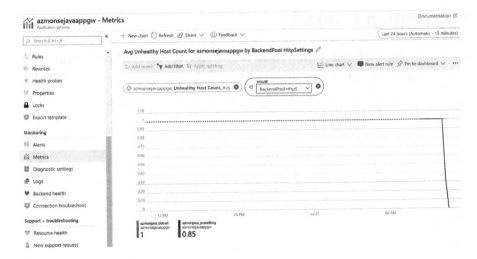

Figure 4-33. *Unhealthy host count metrics*

To enable performance and firewall log monitoring, configure the diagnostics settings from Application gateway ➤ Monitoring ➤ diagnostic setting ➤ Add diagnostic setting (Figure 4-34).

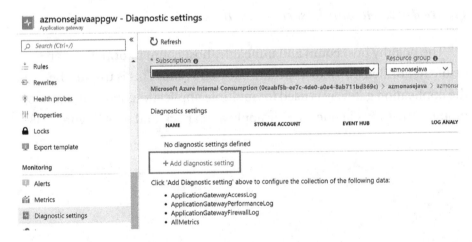

Figure 4-34. *Add diagnostic settings*

Configure the diagnostics information to be sent to a storage account, stream it to Event Hub, or send to a log analytics workspace. In this example, we are sending the Performance log and Firewall log data to the log analytics workspace (Figure 4-35).

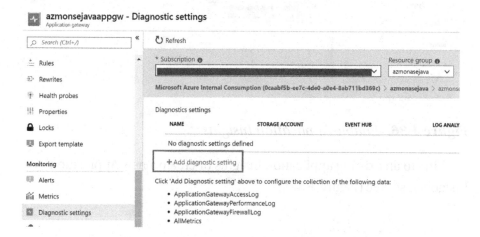

Figure 4-35. *Application gateway diagnostic settings*

Application Insights

Application Insights should be included in the architecture for monitoring of your app service. It can be done using the Application Insights Agent, which is from the Azure portal and ensures a minimum level of monitoring.

Browse to the application ➤ settings ➤ Application Insights and click on "Turn on Application Insights" (Figure 4-36).

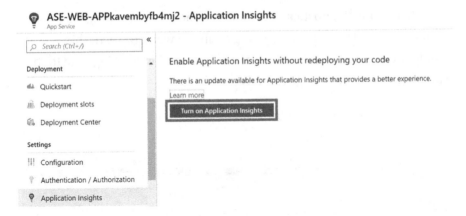

Figure 4-36. *Enable Application Insights*

Link to an existing application Insights or create a new Application Insights resource (Figure 4-37).

Figure 4-37. *Select/Create Application Insights*

Additional settings such as configuration of the collection level, Profiler, SnapShot debugger, etc., can also be configured from this window (Figure 4-38).

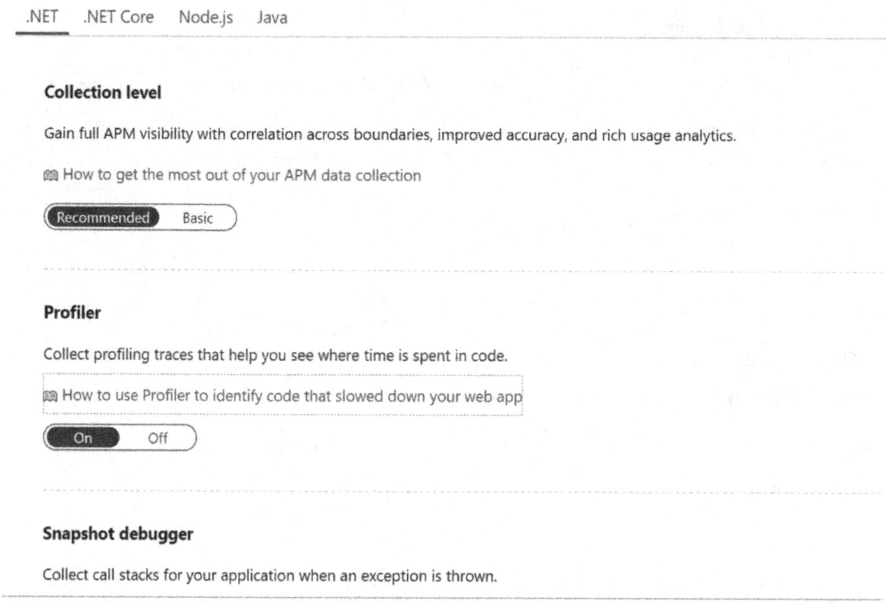

.NET   .NET Core   Node.js   Java

Collection level

Gain full APM visibility with correlation across boundaries, improved accuracy, and rich usage analytics.

📖 How to get the most out of your APM data collection

(Recommended)   (Basic)

Profiler

Collect profiling traces that help you see where time is spent in code.

📖 How to use Profiler to identify code that slowed down your web app

(On)   (Off)

Snapshot debugger

Collect call stacks for your application when an exception is thrown.

Figure 4-38. *Application Insights additional settings configuration*

Click apply to complete the configuration of Application Insights.

You can also manually instrument the code by using Application insights SDK from an IDE like Visual Studio. It is recommended if additional customizations are required where you want to monitor events or dependencies using custom API calls.

Live Metrics from Application Insights is another useful feature that helps you monitor the metrics and performance counters of applications in real time. It is a noninvasive method for live monitoring of your application. Live Metrics needs the latest version of Application Insights SDK and the Microsoft.ApplicationInsights.PerfCounterCollector package to be installed in your webapp. Unlike other metrics that are aggregated over minutes, Live Metrics data (Figure 4-39) is displayed within the duration of 1 second. It is an on-demand monitoring mechanism where the live streaming starts when you open the tab. It does not persist data in storage or log analytics and it is free of charge.

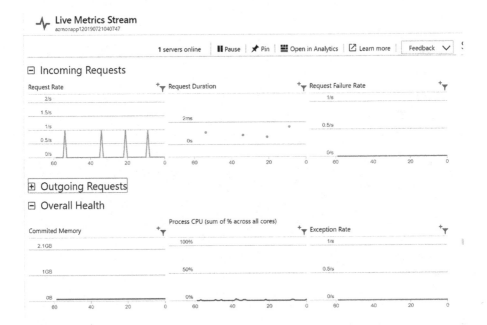

Figure 4-39. *Live Metrics Stream*

Monitoring Multi-Region WebApplication

Let us consider the sample architecture of a multi-region web application that uses Traffic manager for DNS-based load balancing (Figure 4-40).

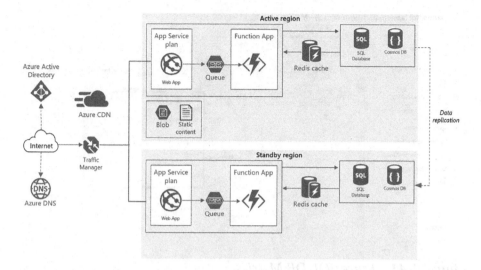

Figure 4-40. *Multi-region web application sample architecture*

As established in the planning section, monitoring will be configured for the following components. Other components like app service plan, storage, etc., are have already been covered in the previous section.

Components	Monitoring Configuration
Azure SQl DB	Basic metrics
	Errors
	QueryStoreRuntimeStatistics
	QueryStoreWaitStatistics
Azure Traffic Manager	Queries by endpoint returned
	Endpoint status by EndPoint

Azure SQl DB

The basic metrics for SQl DB are available from SQl DB ➤ Performance ➤ metrics (Figure 4-41).

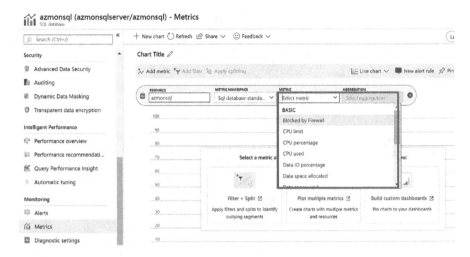

Figure 4-41. *Azure SQL DB Metrics*

We will also configure the SQL performance logs to be sent to the Log analytics workspace for centralized monitoring. From the SQL database settings ➤ Monitoring ➤ Diagnostic settings, add the Diagnostics settings and select the identified logs (Figure 4-42).

- Basic metrics: These metrics contain information like DTU/CPU percentage, limit, data read and log write percentage, firewall connections, etc.

- QueryStoreRuntimeStatistics: Information on CPU usage and query duration statistics during query runtime.

- QueryStoreWaitStatistics:Gives insights on what aspects the queries are being waited on, that is, CPU, Locking, log, etc.

- Errors: These metrics give insights on SQL errors that occur in the database.

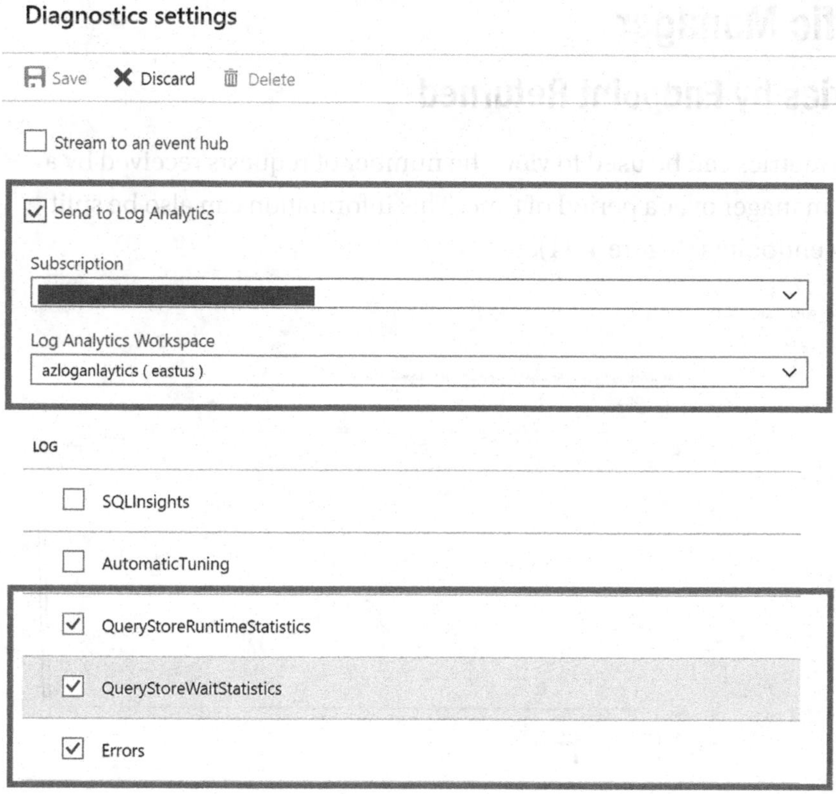

Diagnostics settings

🖫 Save   ✕ Discard   🗑 Delete

☐ Stream to an event hub

☑ Send to Log Analytics

Subscription

[▓▓▓▓▓▓▓▓▓▓▓▓▓▓▓]   ⌄

Log Analytics Workspace

azloganlaytics (eastus)   ⌄

LOG

☐ SQLInsights

☐ AutomaticTuning

☑ QueryStoreRuntimeStatistics

☑ QueryStoreWaitStatistics

☑ Errors

Figure 4-42. *Select Logs*

To view the data and gain additional insights, you can add the solution named Azure SQL Analytics (Preview) in Azure Log analytics (Figure 4-43).

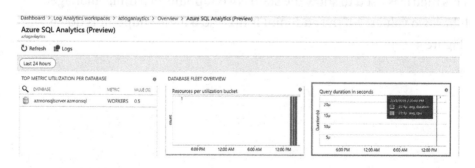

Figure 4-43. *Azure SQL Analytics*

Traffic Manager

Queries by Endpoint Returned

These metrics can be used to view the number of requests received by a traffic manager over a period of time. This information can also be split across endpoints (Figure 4-44).

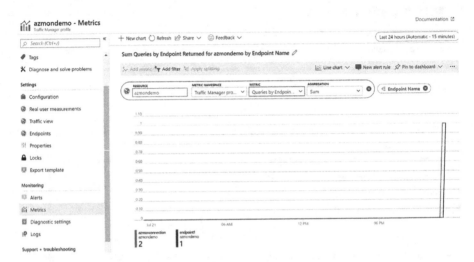

Figure 4-44.   *Queries by endpoint-returned metrics*

Endpoint Status by Endpoint

This metric is used to show the status of endpoints of a traffic manager. It has two values: 1 if the endpoint is up, and 0 if the endpoint is down (Figure 4-45).

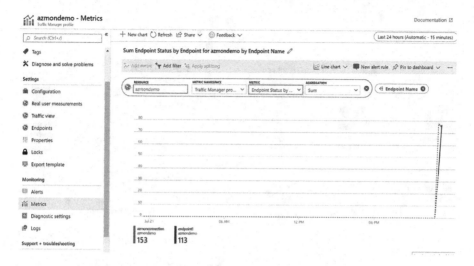

Figure 4-45. *Endpoint status filtered by endpoint Name*

Monitoring of Container-Based Microservices

Let us consider a typical AKS deployment architecture as shown next for this use case (Figure 4-46).

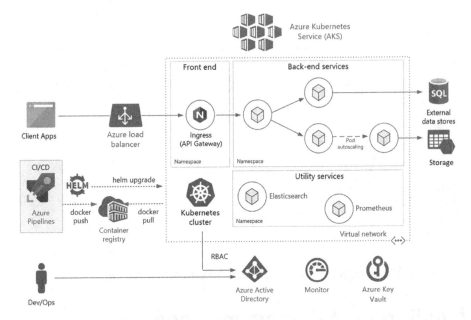

Figure 4-46. *AKS Architecture*

As established in the planning section, monitoring will be configured for the following components.

Components	Monitoring Configuration
AKS	Health status
	Performance: Node CPU and Memory utilization
	Container performance monitoring

Azure offers container monitoring through Azure Monitor for container solutions. It collects performance and memory metrics from nodes as well as containers deployed in those clusters. This information is collated and available for review in log analytics. Container monitoring information, which includes inventory, performance, logs, and events – along with

AKS control plane data – is also captured and made available in the Log Analytics workspace. The following information is available from Azure Monitor for containers:

Average processor and memory utilization of containers deployed in AKS clusters;

Identify the location of container and pod to get a better understanding of the container/pod performance;

Monitor cluster behavior under different loads, which helps in capacity planning and future expansion of the cluster;

Configure thresholds and alerts to notify administrators about potential resource bottlenecks. The functionality of Azure Monitor for containers is depicted in the next diagram (Figure 4-47).

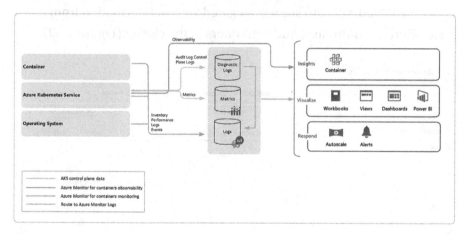

Figure 4-47. *Azure Monitor for containers*

To enable Azure Monitor for containers in your AKS cluster, browse to AKS cluster ➤ Monitoring ➤ Insights. Select the log analytics cluster to which you want to link the cluster and click enable (Figure 4-48).

Figure 4-48.   *Select Log Analytics workspace*

Once enabled, you can see a segregated view of information from Cluster, Nodes, Controllers, and containers in the cluster (Figure 4-49).

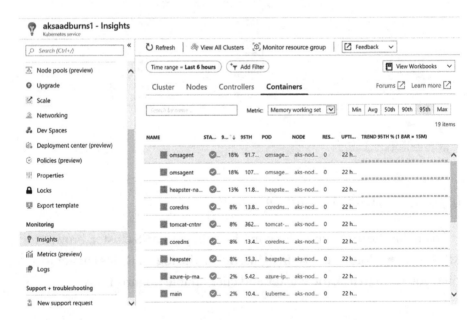

Figure 4-49.   *Azure Monitor for containers sample output*

If you want to do a deeper analysis using container logs, browse to
the log analytics workspace that the AKS cluster was linked to. Browse to
general ➤ Logs and view the logs from "ContainerLog" (Figure 4-50).

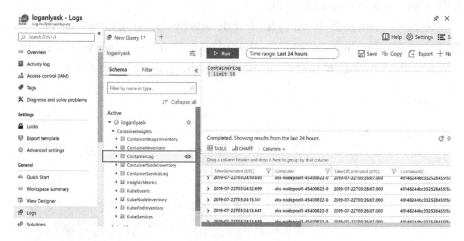

Figure 4-50. *View Container log*

Additional metrics information is available by default from
Monitoring ➤ Metrics (preview) (Figure 4-51).

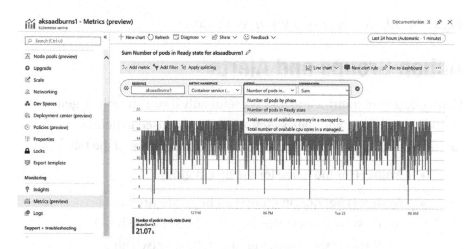

Figure 4-51. *Additional container metrics*

You can view the following information from the Figure 4-51: Number of pods by phase, Number of pods in the ready state, Total amount of memory available in a managed cluster, and Total number of available CPU cores in a managed cluster.

You can even drill down to further details by applying dimensions. For example, for the metrics "Number of pods in ready state," you can drill down to the number of pods in a specific namespace (Figure 4-52).

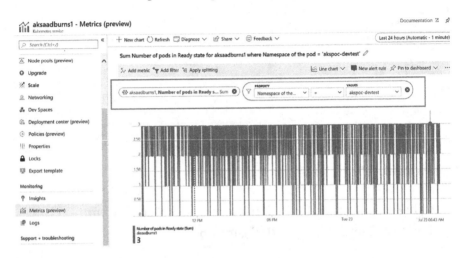

Figure 4-52. *Number of pods in ready state*

Action Groups and Alerts

Configuration of metrics and logs is useful only if you are able to generate alerts in case of any anomalies. Action groups are used to define the notification mechanism for alerts. Action groups consist of the following:

- **Name:** Unique name for the action group;

- **Action type:** Action group can be configured to notify stakeholders through emails, SMS, push notifications, or voice messages. It can also call a logic app, Function, Webhook, Automation runbook, or generate an ITSM ticket;

- **Details:** These are configurations specific to the Action
  type selected.

Action groups will be called during an alert configuration, thereby triggering a notification when an alert condition is met.

To configure Action groups, open Azure Monitor ➤ Alerts ➤ Manage actions ➤ Add action group.

Provide information such as Action group name, Short name to be included in notifications, and the subscription and resource group where the action group will be created. In this, for example, we will trigger an automation runbook using the action group, and hence "Automation Runbook" is selected as the Action type. Click on Edit details to configure the runbook to be used (Figure 4-53).

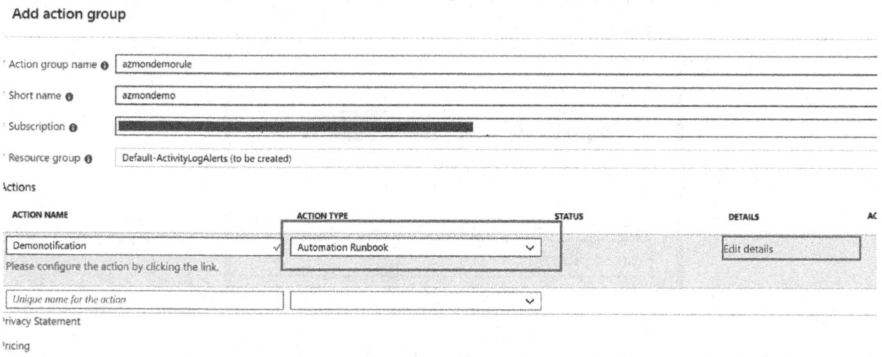

Figure 4-53. Select Action Type

In the Configure runbook tab, select the Runbook source. It can be built in runbook or runbooks created by users. There are built-in runbooks available to perform the following activities: Stop, Restart, Scale up, Scale down, and Remove VM. In this example, we have selected the Scale up VM option. Select a subscription and an automation account in the subscription. All other configurations can be default. Click on Ok. It will take you back to the action group configuration window. Click Ok there to create the action group (Figure 4-54).

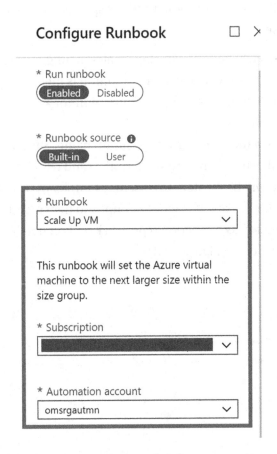

Figure 4-54. *Select Automation Runbook*

Now that an action group is created, let us see how to use the action group in alerts. To create an alert for a VM using collected metrics, browse to the VM ➤ Monitoring ➤ Alerts and Click on the new alert rule. Click on Add under Condition and click on the metrics to be used. In this example, let us create an alert rule based on the CPU percentage (Figure 4-55).

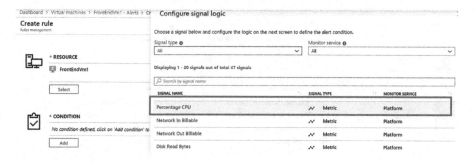

Figure 4-55. *Select signal logic for alert rule*

Configure the alert condition. Here the action group will be generated when the CPU utilization is greater than 80% for 5 minutes (Figure 4-56).

Alert logic

Threshold

| Static | Dynamic |

Operator	* Aggregation type	* Threshold value
Greater than	Average	80

Condition preview

Whenever the percentage cpu is greater than 80 percent

Evaluated based on

* Aggregation granularity (Period)	Frequency of evaluation
5 minutes	Every 5 Minutes

Figure 4-56. *Alert configuration*

The next step is to configure an action in the Action group. Click on Add and select the Action group that we created earlier. Essentially this alert setting scales up the VM to the next available size when the CPU percentage is higher than 80% for 5 minutes (Figure 4-57).

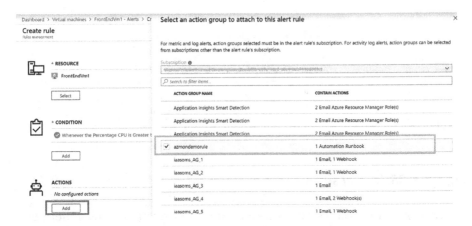

Figure 4-57. *Select action group*

Note   You can add additional action groups to the same rule, for example, to send an email to the IT team so that when the configured condition matches, the IT team is alerted while the VM is also scaled up automatically.

The next step is to set an alert rule name, description, and severity; and then click on "Create Alert rule: to complete the configuration (Figure 4-58).

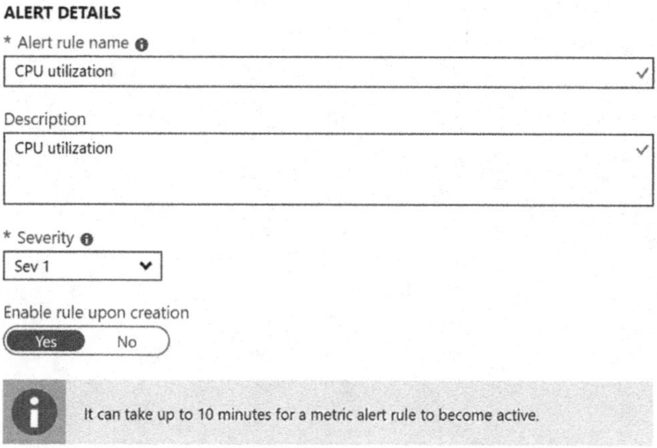

ALERT DETAILS

* Alert rule name ⓘ

| CPU utilization | ✓ |

Description

| CPU utilization | ✓ |

* Severity ⓘ

| Sev 1 | ⌄ |

Enable rule upon creation

(Yes) No

ⓘ It can take up to 10 minutes for a metric alert rule to become active.

Figure 4-58. *Create Alert rule*

Summary

In this chapter, we have reviewed the different phases of implementation of monitoring for cloud-only scenarios: that is, evaluation, planning, and implementation. We also covered the different possible scenarios and implementation details of respective components. Azure Monitoring enables customers to configure alerts based on the monitoring configurations: that is, notifying stakeholders or taking actions such as executing runbooks. The configuration details of the same was also covered in this chapter.

CHAPTER 5

Integration and Hybrid Monitoring

In previous chapters, we looked at Azure Monitor end-to-end monitoring, alerting, insight, and visualization capabilities. We also looked at which features can be leveraged in a given scenario. It is, however, important to realize that enterprises already have invested in and are using existing monitoring tools and security systems for their on-premises IT estate. In order to leverage the existing investment and to achieve the benefits of the cloud, Azure Monitor needs to integrate with these systems. In this chapter, we will look at some of these systems and how Azure Monitor integrates with them. We will also explore a monitoring scenario with Azure resources and some key implementation steps.

To begin with, Figure 5-1 depicts a few key, possible integration tools with Azure Monitor.

© Bapi Chakraborty and Shijimol Ambi Karthikeyan 2019
B. Chakraborty and S. A. Karthikeyan, *Understanding Azure Monitoring*,
https://doi.org/10.1007/978-1-4842-5130-0_5

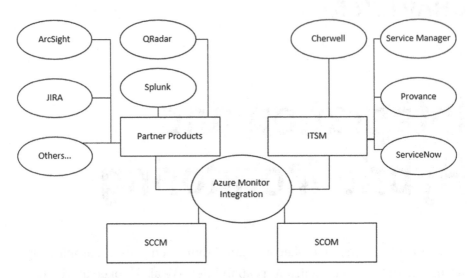

Figure 5-1. *Azure Monitor Integration scenarios*

Let's us now explore some of these integration scenarios and configurations.

Integrate SCOM with Azure Monitor

By connecting System Center Operations Manager (SCOM) to Azure
Monitor, you can leverage cloud scale efficiency and technology value.
Azure Monitor can add value and complements SCOM by collecting,
analyzing, and ND storing the SCOM data. At a high level, the integration
works as follows:

1. You add the type of data you wish to collect using
    Log Analytics "Advanced Settings" as shown in
    Figure 5-2.

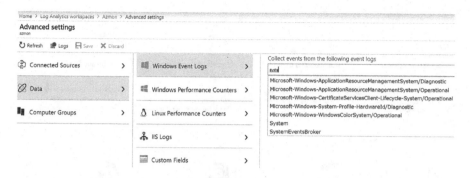

Figure 5-2. *Azure Log Analytics Advanced settings*

2. You add and enable additional solutions in
    your workspace other than agent monitoring
    configurations. This is done using Azure
    Marketplace. Management monitoring solutions
    help in collecting additional data and telemetry
    for specific resources. You can browse all available
    IT and Management Solutions in the Marketplace
    by accessing Solutions service in the Azure portal.
    From your Azure portal home screen, browse to
    "Solutions" and select "MarketPlace" and choose
    "IT & Management Tools." Figure 5-3 shows a few
    available solutions that can be incorporated.

IT & Management Tools > Featured

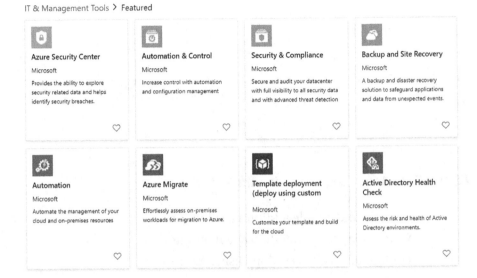

Figure 5-3. *IT and Management Tools on Azure Marketplace*

3. Connect SCOM with Azure Monitor.

4. Deploy the agents to the endpoints or servers and clients.

5. Agents collect data based on configurations.

6. Send data to management server (SCOM) or to the log analytics workspace depending on the type, volume of data, and solutions enabled.

7. The management server sends data to log analytics.

Although the SCOM integration may sound simple enough, the following items need to be kept in mind while designing the solution with SCOM integration:

- If you have systems either on-premises and/or on Azure that are monitored but without direct internet connectivity, you should consider utilizing "Log Analytics Gateway." The log analytics gateway is a system connected to the internet and communicates with the agent to receive and send configurations and data to the workspace.

- The SCOM server does not send data to a data warehouse.

- The management server caches data locally if it loses connectivity with Azure Monitor.

- Another management server in the group resumes a connection with Azure Monitor if the management server is offline due to planned or unplanned maintenance/outage.

- Which server on Azure will be monitored by SCOM and which ones with a log analytics agent directly using a planform extension.

A Sample Integration Scenario

Next is a simple scenario that seeks to explain the integration with the use of Figure 5-4: SCOM and Azure Monitor integration.

1. The on-premises infrastructure is connected to the Azure virtual network using either an ExpressRoute or site-to-site connectivity.

2. All existing on-premises infrastructure is monitored by SCOM and data is collected by the management server.

135

3. All Azure IaaS workloads are monitored, and data is sent directly to Log Analytics in Azure Monitor.

4. The management server is connected to Log Analytics in Azure Monitor.

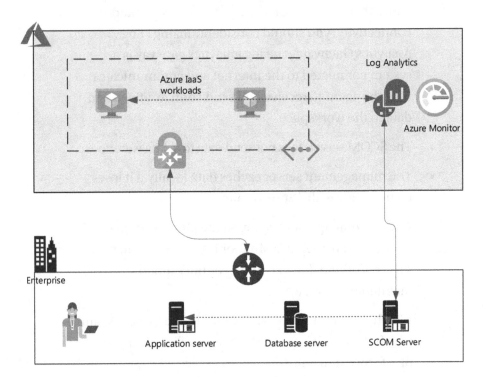

Figure 5-4. *SCOM and Azure Monitor integration*

Prerequisites

Here are the prerequisites:

- An existing Log Analytics workspace;

- Minimum rights as a Log Analytics Contributor role;

- Supported regions. This may change over a period. Refer to the latest Microsoft documentation for any addition or changes in the list;

    - Japan East

    - East US

    - West US 2

    - West Central US

    - West Europe

    - UK South

    - Canada Central

    - Australia South East

    - South East Asia

    - Central India

- SCOM 2016 or later, SCOM 2012 SP1 UR6 or later, and SCOM 2012 R2 UR2 OR later;

- All agents must meet the minimum support requirements;

- Always visit the Microsoft documentation page for any changes or updates in `https://docs.microsoft.com/en-us/azure/azure-monitor/platform/om-agents#prerequisites`.

Simple Implementation Steps

It is assumed that data sources and solutions are already configured and agents are already deployed to the required servers. The steps that follow only explain the connectivity establishment.

1. In the SCOM management server console, browse to "Administration" workspace and choose "Azure Log Analytics" and then "Connection" as shown in Figure 5-5. Click "Register to Log Analytics" in the Administration workspace of the SCOM management console.

Figure 5-5. *Getting started page for register SCOM with Log Analytics*

2. Log in to your subscription and close the subscription and the workspace of which to connect to.

3. Once the connectivity completes successfully, you will be able to add computers, computer groups, reconfigure the log analytics workspace, and configure a Proxy server from the same Connections page as shown in Figure 5-6. It is important to note that if you have a proxy server to connect to the internet in your environment, you need to configure winhttp proxy settings on the SCOM server before you perform these steps. The proxy configuration

option that you see in the next image is not available
before the connectivity at the time of writing this
step. The command is given here:

```
netsh winhttp set proxy <proxyservername>:
<portnumber>
```

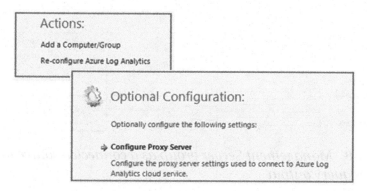

Figure 5-6. *Additonal configuration for SCOM integration with Log
Analytics*

4. Validate the connectivity by checking the
    Management Server Group name in the advanced
    settings of the Log analytics workspace on the Azure
    portal as shown in Figure 5-7.

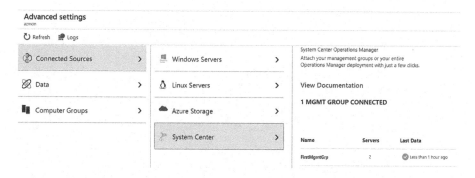

Figure 5-7. *Management Server group as a connected source in Log
Analytics*

You can also run a query to check the agents reporting to log analytics through the management server. Notice the Category column of Figure 5-8.

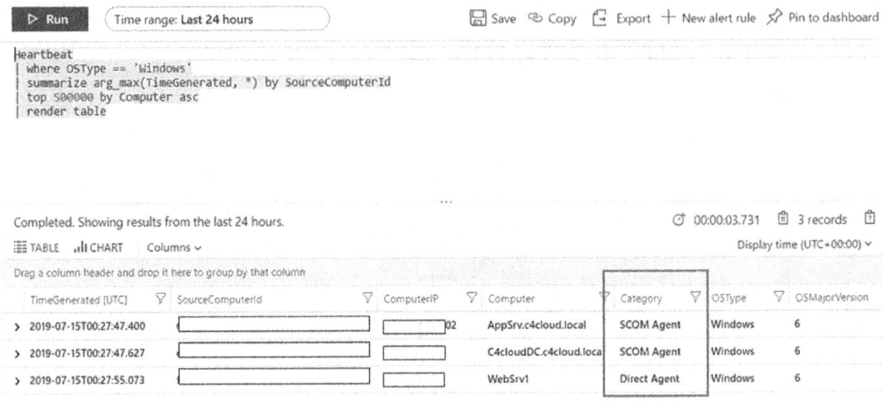

Figure 5-8. *Management Server group as a connected source in Log Analytics query output*

Alternatively, you may also verify the integration by checking the workspace ID in the "Authentication Service URI" section as shown in Figure 5-9 from the SCOM management Console – Monitoring workspace.

Detail View

Health Service properties of AppSrv.c4cloud.local

Display Name	AppSrv.c4cloud.local
Full Path Name	AppSrv.c4cloud.local**AppSrv.c4cloud.local**
Authentication Name	
Maximum Queue Size	104857600
Maximum Size Of All Transferred Files	
Request Compression	True
Create Listener	False
Port	5723
Is Root Health Service Emulator	False
Is Management Server	False
Is Agent	True
Is Gateway	False
Is Manually Installed	False
Installed By	
Install Time	7/14/2019 10:59:34 PM
Version	10.19.10014.0
Action Account Identity	SYSTEM
Send Heartbeats to Management Servers	True
Heartbeat Interval (seconds)	60
Managed Through Active Directory	False
Proxying Enabled	False
Patch List	
Agent communication protocol	
Agent initiates connection to parent agents	
Authentication service URI	

Figure 5-9. *SCOM management Console "Authentication Service URI"*

Removing Integration

Removing the integration, however, is not as easy as connection. This
is because of several references created in the management group,
interdependencies created in management packs, and added complexity
created due to addition of solutions added and its related management
packs. Though we are not covering the steps in detail here, the high-level
process includes the following:

1. Remove the SCOM management packs running the
    PowerShell commands.

    Get-SCOMManagementPack -name "*Advisor*"
    | Remove-SCOMManagementPack -ErrorAction
    SilentlyContinue;

141

Get-SCOMManagementPack -name
"*IntelligencePack*" | Remove-
SCOMManagementPack -ErrorAction
SilentlyContinue;

2. Remove the dependencies of any other
   management packs by running the script available
   on TechNet script center.

   https://gallery.technet.microsoft.com/
   scriptcenter/Script-to-remove-a-84f6873e

3. Remove the reference of the management group
   from Log analytics workspace Advanced Settings ➤
   Connected sources. The remove button will only be
   visible if no sync occurs for 14 days.

4. Delete the below connectors by using a PowerShell
   script available on the Microsoft documentation
   site: https://docs.microsoft.com/en-us/azure/
   azure-monitor/platform/om-agents.

   • Microsoft System Center Advisor

   • Microsoft System Center Advisor Internal

You will need to add these two management packs from the source
media if you want to integrate SCOM with Azure Monitor in the future.

With SCOM and Azure monitor integrated and all data being in Log
Analytics, you now have the power of the cloud for all your IT estate in the
cloud as well of that on-premises.

Integrate SCCM with Azure Monitor

Consider a scenario wherein you wish to address a group of systems in Azure Monitor and in Azure Automation based on the Configuration Manager device collection; you need to see all device collections in Azure Monitor and reference them. This is made possible by connecting the Configuration Manager with Azure Monitor.

You can direct a log query in Azure Log Analytics on a group of computers, thereby limiting the results only to a targeted member in certain scenarios, for example, Upgrade analysis, etc. You can build a targeted list either by using a defined log query or by importing groups of computers from various sources. Then you can reference them in Azure Monitor or Azure Automation or review their collection data in Log Analytics. You can create a computer group using either of the following methods in Log Analytics Advanced Settings. Please refer to Figure 5-10 for configuration settings:

- Log query

- Log search API

- Active Directory groups

- Configuration Manager collections

- WSUS groups target

Figure 5-10. *SCCM integration with Azure Monitor Log Analytics*

If your organization if already using System Center Configuration Manager, you can easily import Configuration Manager collection memberships. You can do so via Configuration Manager's built-in OMS Connector or the Log Analytics Connector. The steps broadly include the following:

1. Creating an Azure AD identity as Web API/Web App.

2. Provide rights to the identity to Azure Monitor using "Access Control (IAM)."

3. In the Configuration Manager Administration console, add a connection to the OMS/Azure Monitor; use the App secret, client ID that was created.

4. Install the Log analytics agent to the SCCM service connection point site role server.

5. Import the collections from the SCCMas computer groups in Azure Monitor.

6. View and use data in Azure Monitor as required.

This is a change management step and creating an Identity can be an additional change management activity. As an architect or consultant, the timeline that goes into this needs to be considered. Actually, this can be handled as a two-step activity: one for the identity creation and rights assignment and the second one for the actual SCCM connection configuration with Azure Monitor. Considering the fact that both these two sets of activities may be performed by two different sets of users, it makes life easier to achieve. The first one most likely will be performed by an Identity team or an existing operational team at the enterprise; the second sets of configurations may be performed either by an operational team with System center access and/or a project team who is implementing Azure Monitoring capabilities and integrations.

Monitoring Azure Tenant

Identity is the new perimeter. With the expansion and adoption of the public cloud, identity has become a central point for data access authorization security. Gone are the days when a network used to be a security perimeter. It still exists. However, the cloud has enabled new scenarios. With more remote workers, bring-your-own-device work culture, and work-from-anywhere concepts and accessibility of application and data securely from anywhere in the world have caused user identities to be closely monitored. Azure Active Directory is a tenant-wide service. All on-cloud identities or usage of synced (hybrid) identity helps to achieve a truly global platform with single sign-on capabilities, advanced security, multifactor authentication, point-in-time access, conditional access, group-based access control, etc. In this section we will explore the following:

- Microsoft Azure tenant monitoring (Azure Active Directory) Logs and reports and what kind of data they store;

- How to configure and obtain them;

- Important factors that help design decisions and planning;

- How to gather insights.

Understanding the Logs

Azure Active Directory monitoring provides the below reports and logs.

- Security Reports

    - Users flagged for risk: Provides overview of user accounts that might have been compromised.

    - Risky Sign-Ins / Risk Events: Events logged indicating that the activity may be performed by an illegitimate user or by someone who is not the actual owner of the user account.

- Activity Reports

    - Audit Logs: Provides history of tasks performed by the tenant. Very useful for audit trail purposes and for analyzing any unexpected event that might have taken place.

    - Sign-ins: Sign-in reports can help identify the user who has performed the activity reported by the Audit log.

All versions of Azure AD Free, Basic, Premium 1, and Premium 2 provide Security reports that include flagged users and risky sign-ins. The details and granularity vary based on the version. All of the reports' data are also available via REST-based APIs to be accessible from various tools and programming languages. You can code using your own tool and programming language, and through REST APIs these reports' data can be accessed.

While addressing any functional, nonfunctional requirements, or compliance and security needs, these reports can be utilized in various ways.

Enabling Azure AD Diagnostics

Depending on the requirement, the Azure AD logs can be streamed either to a Storage account, Event Hub, or to Log Analytics. You need to have either a Global Administrator or Security Administrator rights configure these settings. Figure 5-11 shows the available Azure AD diagnostic settings.

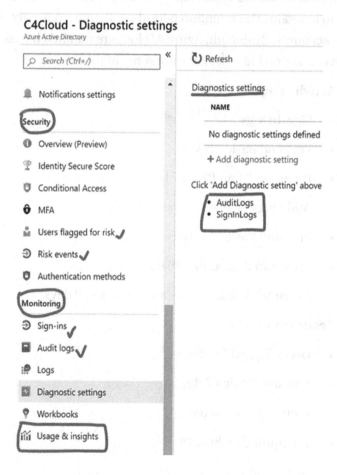

Figure 5-11. *Azure AD diagnostic settings*

The configuration can be done by logging onto the Azure portal ➤ Azure Active Directory ➤ Monitoring Blade ➤ Diagnostic settings ➤ Add diagnostic settings. From this page you can either archive logs to a storage account, stream to Event Hub, or send to log analytics.

Use Cases

Archive Logs to a Storage Account

Use this method to choose which logs you need to archive and for logs that you need do to retain. The retention period configuration is only available for storage accounts. By default, Azure AD logs are retained based on the Azure AD version and log type. Here are some of the details:

- **Activity Logs:**
  - Sign-In logs
  - Free and basic - NA
  - Premium P1 an P2 - 30 days
  - Audit logs
  - Free and basic - 7 days
  - Premium P1 and P2 - 30 days
  - Azure MFA usage data - all versions - 30 days
- **Security Logs:**
  - Users flagged for risk
  - Free and Basic - 7 days
  - Premium P1 - 30 days
  - Premium P2 - 90 days
  - Risky Sign-ins

- Free and Basic - 7 days

- Premium P1 - 30 days

- Premium P2 - 90 days

Route to Event Hub

By routing Azure AD logs to an Event Hub, you can integrate them with your existing SIEM systems (e.g., Splunk, Sumologic, QRadar, etc.). With all your SIEM-managed data and Identity data together, you can easily analyze, corelate, and derive richer insights from your environment. Routing to Event Hub also enables you to write your own tooling to read data from Event Hub and gain insight the way you want.

Stream Data to Log Analytics

Log analytics can help by storing, retrieving, analyzing, and correlating all audit and sign-in logs. You can create your own dashboards and views or use any existing prebuilt views. You can perform tasks that will help gain additional information and resolve any critical issues. Here are a few examples:

- Compare and contrast logs against Azure Security Center logs and Alerts to identify a potential security issue;

- Users sign-in failure incidents and on a specific timeline;

- Take various remediation actions for risky users;

- Identify and remediate user accounts having unusual activities;

- Remediate a O365 user account if compromised by enabling mailbox auditing, resetting password, reconfiguring delegation, mail forwarding, etc.

149

Figure 5-12 depicts the various Azure AD diagnostic settings storage and retention use cases already discussed.

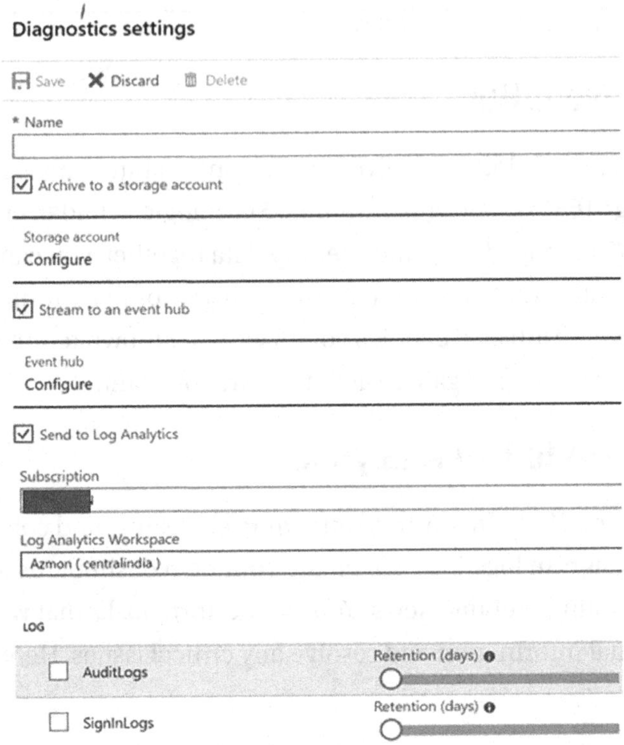

Figure 5-12. *Azure AD diagnostic settings retention for analysis*

Note   You will notice that Users flagged for risk and Risky Events can be downloaded as Reports, whereas Audit Logs and Sign-In Logs can be streamed or routed using one of the methods mentioned earlier.

Reporting Data Latencies

Different types of Azure AD reports and logs take different amounts of time to appear on the Azure portal. This is important to consider while designing the solution and to understand the expected outcome of it. Though it is possible that these values may change and become more real time over a period of time, one should review these values on Microsoft official documentation every time before designing and planning a solution.

- **Security Logs:**
  - Users flagged for risk and Risky Sign-ins
  - Maximum - 2 hours; Average - 15 mins
  - Risk Events
  - Depends on various events - 2 to 8 hours maximum
- **Activity Reports:**
  - Audit and Sign-in Logs - 2 to 5 minutes

Important Factors Designing Azure AD Monitoring and Reporting Solution

Next is a nonexclusive list of items that we should consider and define while we are designing a monitoring solution around identity and its integration with various tools.

- Are you planning and designing for your own infrastructure or for your customer?
- Are you a managed service provider, and do you handle multiple customers?

- How many tenants do you have to monitor, and what are the data governance requirements?

- Are you using a shared tenant or the same tenant used by several customers or internal departments? Are there specific requirements for each of them?

- What is your log analytics Architecture?

- Central: Single log analytics workspace managed by service providers for all/various customers. It can also be a single Log Analytics workspace for all your business units or departments and their projects.

- Distributed: Each customer has their own tenant and log analytics workspace. Different workspaces are based on business unit or department, application, projects, or workload.

- Hybrid: Each department or customer has their own workspace, and analytics is performed in another central workspace.

- Do you need to Archive reports for compliance and Auditing? If yes, for how long?

- Do you need to integrate logs with an existing SIEM system?

- Who should have access to such data?

- Who should be able to view and access Security reports and Activity logs?

- What is the Security, compliance, operational, and governance requirements for monitoring?

- What are the monitoring requirements? What do you want to monitor?

- Have you already identified and established prerequisites?

- What report formats and information are required and at what intervals?

- What visualization, dashboards, and reporting tools are to be used?

- In what scenarios should alerts to be configured, and who should be notified and how?

- Is there a requirement to create a security, operational, or problem incident to be raised with ITSM integration?

- What are the roles and responsibilities of the Global administrators, Security administrators, or any other custom roles in the organization?

- Is there a need to create a custom role? What rights are required? What rights are to be delegated?

- Have you considered log reporting latencies while designing the solution and incident response?

- Define runbook (a list of predefined tasks) for each common identity, security, operational incident; and who is responsible to act on those?

- What activities and processes should be automated?

Like any other monitoring solution, we should closely consider the overall life cycle of tenant monitoring with respect to collect, store, analyze, monitor, and visualize reporting. This model always helps to create a robust, scalable, secured, reusable, available, and reliable while designing.

High-Level Constructs of Azure AD Monitoring

Figure 5-13 summarizes and depicts the overall Azure AD monitoring constructs. We have already discussed the various logs and data available; how to monitor them; and how to enable monitoring and integration with Azure and non-Azure external services, for example, SIEM systems and various considerations and factors while designing and planning an Azure AD monitoring solution.

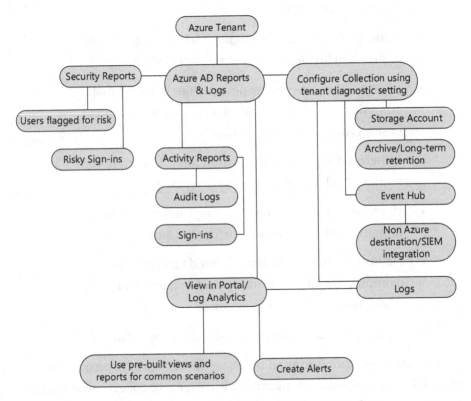

Figure 5-13. *Various constructs of Azure AD monitoring*

Integration with Existing Security Information and Event Management (SIEM) Systems

The importance of Security Intelligence for your datacenter infrastructure is well known. We are not going to discuss that here. In this section, we will be looking at the different scenarios to integrate the security and diagnostic logs generated by Azure and its resources into different SIEM systems. We will also look some of the partner solutions on how to integrate Azure resource logs. We will explore Splunk as an example. However, designing, sizing, scalability, and high availability of the SIEM systems are not in the scope of this discussion.

The following can be possible scenarios involving Azure on how the workloads and SIEM system are located.

Workload Location	SIEM Location	Comment
Azure	Azure	There is a possibility that the SIEM system is hosted by someone else or by you. There may be routing/connectivity between the two locations or not connected at all (except internet)
Azure	On-Premises	Common scenario. It is possible that the SIEM system is hosted by someone else (incumbent/ service provider) or by yourself. There may be routing/connectivity between the two locations or not connected at all (except by the internet)
On-Premises	Azure	This may not be a very common scenario but possible. Customer may look to host a newly planned SIEM system on the cloud

Factors to Remember

Here are a few items that we should keep in mind while designing, deploying, and integrating an SIEM system with Azure Monitor:

- Cloud resource – it can be a service, an Azure resource (e.g., Network, Load Balancer, Storage, Network Security group), a Virtual Machine instance (VM, Web and Worker roles) either hosted on Azure or any other Cloud service provider hosting the cloud: for example, AWS.

- Each service may generate different types of logs; the logs can be of different formats.

- Different SIEM systems may support different file formats and integrations.

- Different SIEM systems may support only specific Services or Log types.

- Current product (SIEM) maturity and road map for adopting Azure Monitor Logs.

Basics

Now, let us cover a little bit of how the basics are involved.

The Logs

What are the different types of logs available, and how do we enable them?

Azure produces extensive logging for every service. These logs are categorized as the following:

- Control/Management logs that give visibility into the Azure Resource Manager CREATE, UPDATE, and DELETE operations.

- Data Plane logs that give visibility into the events raised when using an Azure resource. An example is the Windows Event log – security and application logs in a virtual machine.

We can enable these Logs either by PowerShell, using Azure Diagnostics SDK and Visual Studio, from the Azure portal's diagnostic's settings or by using a JSON template incorporating the diagnostics extension.

The resource-specific logs can be enabled either at the time when we deploy the resource or anytime later by using the appropriate method.

There Are Different Services and Resources

The collection methods and type of logs are different.

Various Azure resources emit different logs, for example. VMs will have Event viewer logs and other performance metrics; storage will have performance metrics and access logs; the load balancer and the Network Security Group will emit other sets of logs. The collection method may be differently based in each case. We will discuss them for each type and formats in our upcoming discussions.

Storing the Logs

How do we store the logs? In what format and where in different scenarios do we store them?

We can either store these logs in an Azure Storage account (tables, blobs) or Event Hubs, etc. It may be Event logs forwarded to a collector system. Hence, the logs, data generated by Azure resources, can be XML, CSV, Evtx, TXT, or JASON based. We need to make sure to store them effectively and so that it is easily accessible and interpretable by the different SIEM system.

Required Tools

What tools are required to ingest/stream/copy/export the logs into the SIEM systems?

Azure has its own set of tools enabling these logs to be either Streamed; exported into the SIEM system; or Converted into a standard format, for example, JSON that can be fed into the SIEM system. The Azure log integrator (currently deprecated) is such a tool. Microsoft now recommends vendor-specific connectors for collecting data from Event Hub.

Data Flow Architecture

Microsoft recommends using SIEM vendor's connector to integrate Azure Monitor logs into it. Initially, Azure Log Integrator was introduced to simplify ingesting Azure resource logs into existing SIEM systems. During the evolution phases of the log integrator, the data had to be either exported or stored into a storage account or to tables as necessary. The SIEM systems then, with the help of Azure log integrator and its connector, read from the storage account and streamed data into it.

Now, with Azure Monitor being able to stream data into Event Hub, SIEM vendors can write connectors to read logs directly from the Event Hub. The Azure log integrator was already deprecated in June 2019 and download is now disabled. Some of the leading SIEM vendors already produce their own sets of connectors. We will look at Splunk and its add-on connector as an example. There may already be a newer version of the connector available, and we encourage you to investigate this.

Figure 5-14 shows various ways to integrate with on-premises SIEM systems using a high-level Data flow diagram for better understanding.

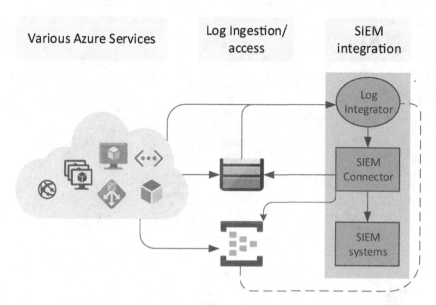

Figure 5-14. *Azure Monitor and SIEM integration Data flow integration*

The New Architecture

Figure 5-15 depicts how an on-premises SIEM system can be integrated with Azure Monitor via Event Hub. In this scenario, we have an on-premises environment that uses an existing SIEM system. The Azure IaaS deployment is connected using an Expressroute connectivity. There are IaaS and PaaS deployments involving Azure App services and Azure SQL databases. The Azure resources logs are streamed into an Event Hub. The diagnostic logs and Activity Logs are configured to ingest data into Event Hub. The on-premises SIEM system reads the data from the Event Hub using its connector and integrates itself to perform the necessary security and event management analysis. All existing on-premises systems are already configured to ingest data into the SIEM system either via an Event forwarder or collector system or through an agent installed on the systems.

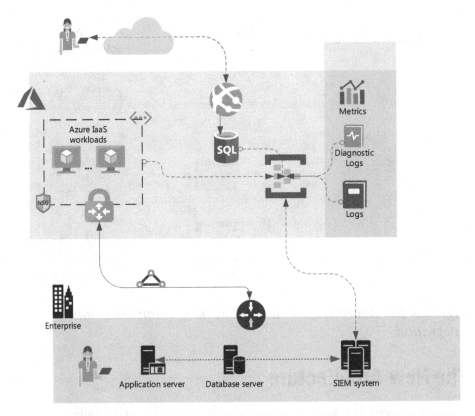

Figure 5-15. *Azure Monitor and on-premises SIEM integration high-level design*

Since Azure Event Hub has become the soul of SIEM integration, it is important to ensure it is set up correctly. Here are a few things to consider:

- Always create a standard namespace (a namespace is a logical collection of Event Hubs that share the same policy);

- Configure Event Hub to scale automatically based on throughput requirements;

- Microsoft recommends starting with four partitions if you are unsure of consumption;

- Continue to use default consumer group unless you are using multiple tools;

- Microsoft recommends data retention for at least 7 days. This will work as a temporary storage of data in case SIEM system goes offline for a few days;

- Configure your on-premises firewall rules to allow outbound 5671 and 5672.

Supported Logs

While designing your overall monitoring strategy and integration, the existing capabilities of Azure resources that can stream data into Event Hub should also be considered. Here are the various types of data that can be ingested into Event Hub.

- Azure Tenant data - Azure AD activity logs including Sign-In logs and Audit logs. AAD security reports to be viewed separately.

- Subscription monitoring data – Activity Logs.

- Azure resource-specific diagnostic logs and Metrics (for supported services. Not all services have diagnostic integration or specific metrics that can be ingested.). Review the latest Azure documentation to gather details.

- Guest OS data: Use a Linux or Windows Diagnostic agent to collect monitoring data.

- Application monitoring data with added effort. Since application monitoring data is ingested to Application Insight (with the help of instrumented code with an SDK), you cannot by default route application data to

Event Hub with a simple configuration. You can, however, stream Application Insight data to Event Hub by:

- Setting up a continuous export of app insight data to a storage account;

- Create a timer-triggered logic app that reads data from a storage account and pushes them to Event Hub as a message.

Once all necessary monitoring data from various resources are routed to Event Hub, the SIEM connector can be configured to read from the Event Hub and ingest logs into it. The approach to how each SIEM system may integrate can be a little different.

Integrating Activity Logs with Your Existing SIEM

The capabilities may vary depending on the product and how it integrates. Some SIEM systems can integrate with an Azure Storage account to read data from it and some with an Event Hub; others may do both.

To get the Activity logs into the SIEM system, we will need to export the data from a Storage account or to an Event Hub first. On the Azure portal, browse to Activity logs ➤ Click "Export to Event Hub" option from the Activity log and choose the appropriate storage account or Event Hub. Figure 5-16 explains the steps.

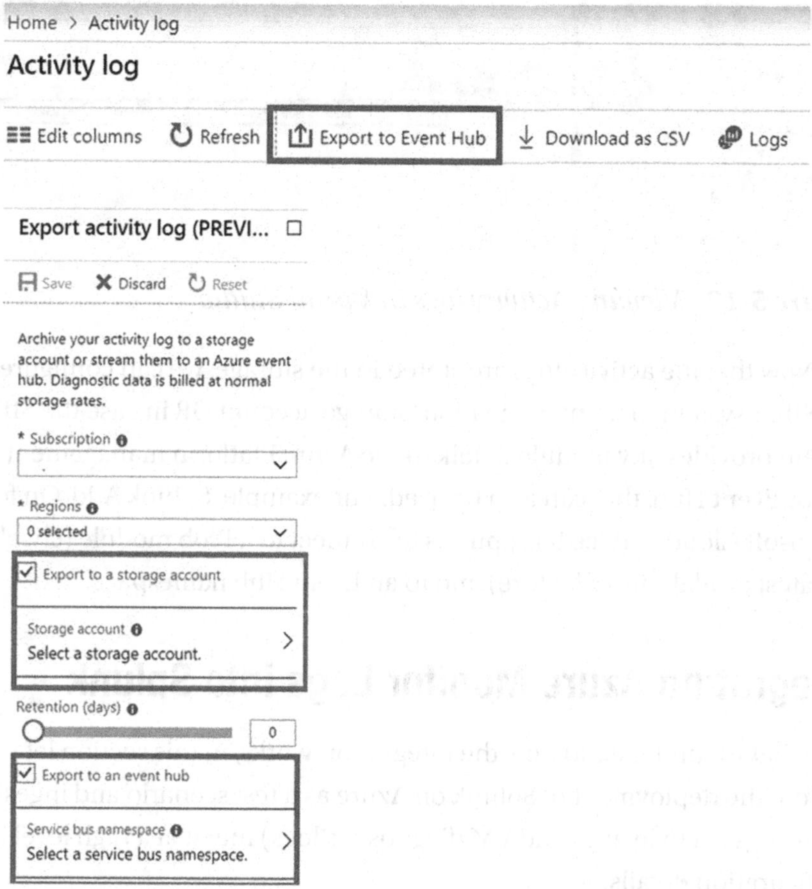

Home > Activity log

Activity log

≣≣ Edit columns   ↻ Refresh   ┌─ 🗁 Export to Event Hub ─┐   ↓ Download as CSV   🔎 Logs

Export activity log (PREVI... □

🖫 Save   ✗ Discard   ↻ Reset

Archive your activity log to a storage
account or stream them to an Azure event
hub. Diagnostic data is billed at normal
storage rates.

* Subscription ❶

[. ⌄]

* Regions ❶

[0 selected ⌄]

☑ Export to a storage account

Storage account ❶   >
Select a storage account.

Retention (days) ❶

○▬▬▬▬▬▬▬▬▬▬   [0]

☑ Export to an event hub

Service bus namespace ❶   >
Select a service bus namespace.

Figure 5-16. *Export Activity logs to Event Hub or Storage account*

This process creates an appropriate Log Profile and stores the data in
a Storage account or Event Hub that can be used to integrate into a SIEM
system.

This data as shown in Figure 5-17 can also be viewed in the Visual
Studio. The data is in the form of a JSON file in a Blob container in the
storage account created.

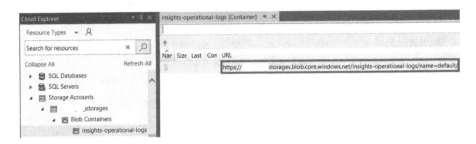

Figure 5-17. *Viewing Activity logs in Visual Studio*

Now that the activity logs are stored in the storage, we can configure
the SIEM system to point to the Blob/storage account OR in case the SIEM
system provides any module to talk to the Azure Platform management
API or Event Hub, that can also be used. For example, Splunk Add-On for
Microsoft Cloud Service has options to connect to a Blob module (check
for latest availability of feature) and to an Event Hub namespace.

Integrating Azure Monitor Logs into Splunk

Now that we understand how the integration works, in this section let us
explore the deployment of Splunk on Azure as a test scenario and ingest
Azure logs (Activity logs and VM diagnostics logs) into it at a high level of
configuration details.

The technical briefing on such deployment can be found on Splunk
documentation here: `https://www.splunk.com/pdfs/technical-briefs/`
`deploying-splunk-enterprise-on-microsoft-azure.pdf`.

For architectural details, please visit: `https://www.splunk.com/`
`blog/2016/02/18/announcing-splunk-enterprise-in-microsoft-`
`azure-marketplace.html`.

By default, when you deploy the ARM template from Azure
Marketplace, you will receive a 60-day trial of Splunk Enterprise Bring-
your-own-license (BYOL) version of Splunk Enterprise. You can choose
either a Single Instance or a Clustered Instance. Figure 5-18 depicts the
Splunk deployment template at the final review stage.

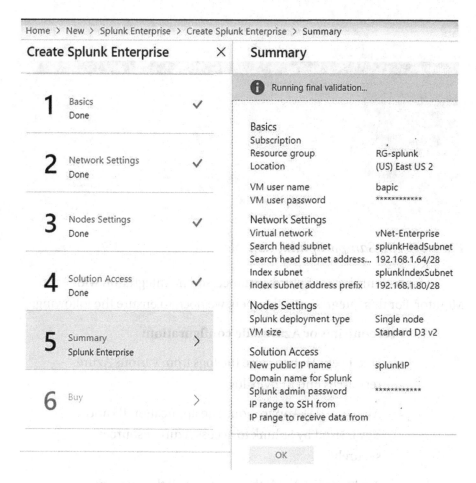

Figure 5-18.   Sample Splunk deployment template on Azure

Once deployed, log in to your Splunk Admin console using its Public IP or DNS name assigned by Azure. You will receive a certificate error since it's a self-signed certificate. You can change it later should you wish to keep the deployment. Figure 5-19 depicts a portion of a sample Splunk console deployed on Azure. For an advanced/production scale Splunk design, deployment, implementation, and management, please visit Splunk documentation and support.

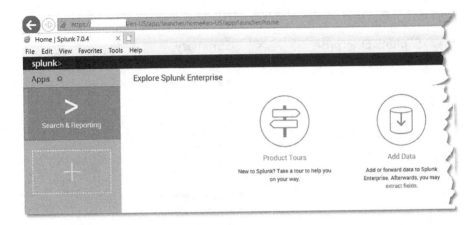

Figure 5-19. *Sample Splunk Console*

So far, we only have a Splunk instance and no integration with Azure Monitor. For this integration to happen, we need to ensure the following:

1. **Prerequisites or Azure side configuration:**

   - One Event Hub to store the logs from various Azure resources and Activity logs.

   - An Azure AD Application. The application ID and Key is used by Splunk to access Azure resources securely.

   - An Azure Key Vault that contains all the relevant secrets, appID, and Event Hub namespace keys.

   For a detailed understanding you can visit:
   https://www.splunk.com/blog/2018/04/20/
   splunking-microsoft-azure-monitor-data-part-
   1-azure-setup.html.

It is also important to understand that the security of the Event Hub and AppIDs are taken care of by securely storing all data and assigning the required lease privileges. As a consultant or architect, these pillars will require additional consideration, discussion, and planning to ensure the required operational or implementation team takes care of them. It is advisable to create a playbook for all such activities with clearly outlined activities to avoid unnecessary confusion and delays. You may also use a script available from Git Hub and process the details mentioned here: `https://github.com/ microsoft/AzureMonitorAddonForSplunk`. It creates all necessary prerequisites for a test environment. You can review and plan your production environment configuration either manually or by updating the script. The script also provides necessary Add-On configuration details that will be used once the add-on is installed. Figure 5-20 shows the configuration inputs while using the PowerShell script for prerequisites.

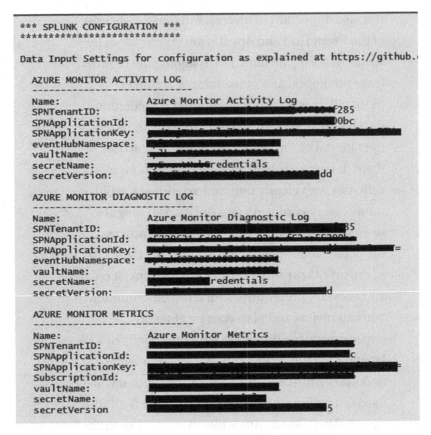

Figure 5-20. *Sample prerequisite script outputs for configuration details*

2. **Installation and configuration of the add-on or Splunk side configuration:**

The add-on can be downloaded from here: https://splunkbase.splunk.com/app/3534/#/ details. Also, you can download from the Git Hub project repository here: https://github. com/microsoft/AzureMonitorAddonForSplunk/ releases. This is a non-Microsoft, community-driven project. Support is community driven as well.

As discussed earlier, other SIEM systems may be configured differently. Each SIEM system may have their own integration methods, tools, and prerequisites.

All you need to do is download the Add-On and save on your system; Log in to Splunk console and Click on "Apps" ➤ Install from File ➤ and point to the file you downloaded (usually an .spl file). Follow the process mentioned on Splunk and Git Hud websites in case you face any issues. Once the Add-On is installed successfully, you will notice the "Azure Monitor" on the Splunk Console under Apps as shown in Figure 5-21.

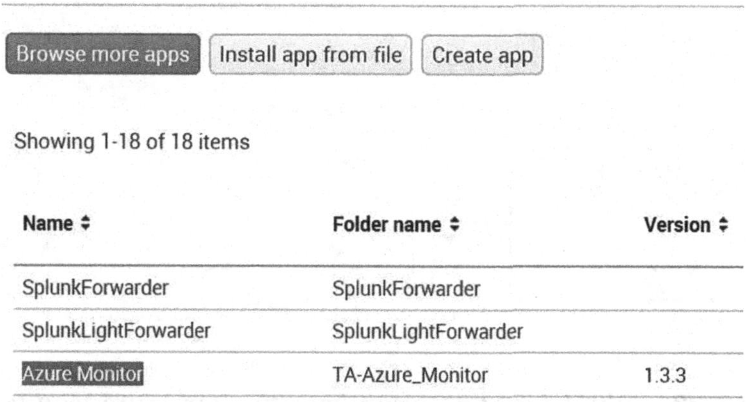

| Browse more apps | Install app from file | Create app |

Showing 1-18 of 18 items

Name ⬍	Folder name ⬍	Version ⬍
SplunkForwarder	SplunkForwarder	
SplunkLightForwarder	SplunkLightForwarder	
Azure Monitor	TA-Azure_Monitor	1.3.3

Figure 5-21. *Azure Monitor Add-On for Splunk*

3. **Configure necessary data source inputs for Splunk:**

Now that basic configurations are done, you can configure necessary data inputs from the Splunk Settings page as shown in Figure 5-22. This configuration uses the outputs from the scripts for each data input type. Splunk uses these data to connect to the Event Hub to gather the necessary data and to normalize, analyze, report, etc.

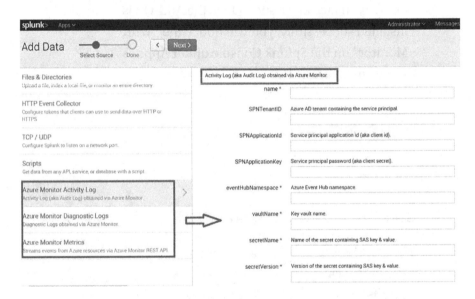

Figure 5-22. Splunk input data configuration for Azure Monitor

4. **Configure Log data to flow into Event Hub**

This is the last step to ensure data flows into Event Hub so that Splunk can read from it. All resources that allow diagnostics data to be streamed into Event Hub should be configured. Once done, data should be searchable and available in Splunk. For example, please refer to the previous section for integrating Activity logs. For a list of services that support Azure diagnostics, logs can be found here: `https://docs.microsoft.com/en-us/azure/azure-monitor/platform/diagnostic-logs-schema`. As for metrics of the Virtual machines, all Virtual machines should be tagged with Metrics: <value> as required.

Scenario Example: Monitoring a Hybrid Environment

In this section we will look at an application deployment that spans across on-premises and Azure resources, and we will explore the various components of application monitoring.

The Environment

An organization named C4cloud has recently adopted Microsoft Azure as their public cloud platforms and deployed one of their business applications. The application is accessed by both internal and external users over the internet. The business application consists of the following components:

- One Application server on-premises;
- Two Azure Virtual machines;
- One storage account;
- One application Gateway;
- One App service hosting a Web App; and
- One Azure SQL database.

The Application

Here are details of the application:

- Data entry users update raw data over a web console hosted on the Application server on-premises. The Application server runs a batch job every one hour and adds additional information to the data and uploads the data to a storage account on Azure. It then calls into an API hosted on the application servers on Azure.

- There are two application servers on Azure deployed in a Virtual network that read the data from the storage account, add additional information, and store it into the SQL database.

- The App Service uses the data from the SQL server to serve to the external users through the Application Gateway. Application gateway is configured in Web Application Firewall mode (prevention). The application also serves as a reporting service.

- There is a site-to-site VPN connection that exists between the on-premises network and the production virtual network on Azure.

- C4Cloud uses an on-premises identity for their application and is integrated with Azure Active Directory.

- C4Cloud uses SCOM for their existing workload monitoring on-premises. However, they are interested in exploring new cloud capabilities.

Figure 5-23 represents the scenario.

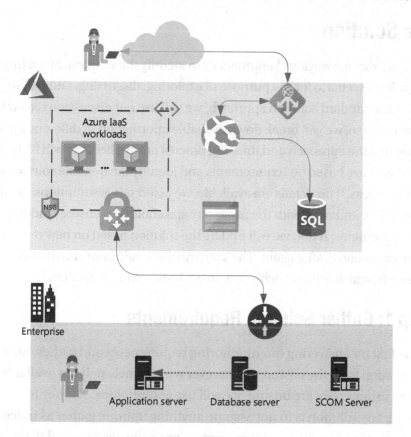

Figure 5-23. C4cloud Application scenario

The Requirements

C4cloud is required to ensure the following:

- All critical application components should be monitored for failures;

- Monitor the application for health, performance, exceptions, availability;

- Support and operations team should be alerted to failures;

- Use an existing solution wherever possible.

The Solution

There are various ways and approaches to identify the solution. Since this is a high-level scenario for the purpose of exploring, discussing, and helping to create a standard solution approach, we will use our discussions so far to achieve it. Also, we will break down available information in different ways to ensure that the approach and thinking process are applied. We will fill in the details we have based on requirements and identify the possible solutions as we progress. If no details are available, we assert our assumptions, create the solution, and work with the necessary stakeholder to ensure it addresses the requirements. If not, we will update the solution based on new or added information and draft it again. The scenario discussed here and the next approach is an attempt to achieve a broad-level solution creation.

Step 1: Gather Solution Requirements

Let us first try answering our monitoring requirements and gather more information from the customer wherever we are unclear. If not available or the customer/we are unsure, we will use assumptions. The key to creating any solution is to not assume anything upfront, gather as much information as possible, and then suggest or assume as required if details are not available. Customers and partners look up to the experts for advice. So, draft and ask more questions if you need to.

Solution Scoping Questions	Responses Based on Available Data
What system do you wish to monitor?	An existing application that is deployed across on-premises and Azure. It includes multiple on-premises and Azure services.
Why do you want to monitor? This drills down to Monitoring scenarios mentioned below in Step 2.	All critical components of the application.

(continued)

Solution Scoping Questions	Responses Based on Available Data
For how long?	Always. To ensure application availability.
Are you troubleshooting an existing issue?	No. Existing deployment and a monitoring solution to be devised.
Which metrics and in which interval do you want to monitor?	Not available. Suggest based on Assumptions; then clarify with stakeholders/customers/ application owners as the case may be.
Which tool and reporting system to use?	Not available. Suggest based on Assumptions; then clarify with stakeholders/customers/ application owners as the case may be.
What action to take if such events are important and requires attention?	Inform the Operations and Support team. No automated action.
Who should be notified of such an event?	Alert Support and Operations teams.
How should they be notified?	Not available. Suggest based on Assumptions; then clarify with stakeholders/customers/ application owners as the case may be.
What actions are expected from that person/team?	This is defined by process. Ensure customer/ application owner already has this in place or uses an existing process and they are aware of the actions.
Is it required to open a support incident or log another event somewhere?	Yes. Since operations team needs to be notified and requires taking action.
What ITSM integration is required?	Not available. Suggest or Assume.

Step 2: What Is the Monitoring Scenario(s)?

Gather the monitoring scenarios based on functional and nonfunctional requirements.

Scenarios	Tick if Applies (X)/Comments
SLA	(No requirement for this scenario)
Auditing & Compliance	(No requirement for this scenario)
Security	(No requirement for this scenario)
Availability	X (the application requires to be up and all failures and exceptions to be reported)
Performance	X (the application requires to be up and all failures and exceptions to be reported)
Usage	(No requirement for this scenario)
Health	X (the application requires to be up and all failures and exceptions to be reported)

Step 3: Remember the Azure Data Life Cycle?

Let us use the life cycle to gather more information and then try to create the solution.

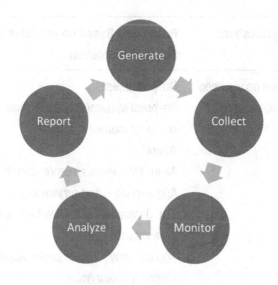

Generate

Logs are generated from various resources. Start with the Anchor.

Solution Scoping Questions	Responses Based on Available Data/ Suggested Solution
What resources do we need to monitor?	**On-premises:** On-prem system/virtual machine **Azure:** Azure VM App Service SQL database App gateway Network connectivity VPN Gateway Application Code Health of all resources Others/Misc: NA for any dependent systems\

(continued)

Solution Scoping Questions	Responses Based on Available Data/ Suggested Solution
What logs and types do we need to capture from each source?	**On-premises:** On-prem system/virtual machine - *events, resource metrics* **Azure:** Azure VM - *events, resource metrics* App Service - *App service logs* SQL database - *SQL Diagnostics, Intelligent performance* App gateway - *Health probe, AppGW diagnostics/analytics* Network connectivity - *NSG diagnostics*, NPM, *traffic analytics* VPN Gateway - *Network watcher, metrics* Application Code - Application Insight logs, · `Azure Health state` - *All above resources* Others/Misc: N/A for any dependent systems
Do all resources generate required data?	Yes

Collect

Once the sources and type of logs are identified, we need to collect and store them.

Solution Scoping Questions	Responses Based on Available Data/ Suggested Solution
Where do we need to store the data to analyze and report?	Log Analytics, Activity Logs, Application Insights
How do you want to configure and collect the logs/data from the sources?	Use Diagnostics settings for the resources to configure log collection to Log analytics or Application Insight
What are the access management requirements for the log's storage location?	Details not available
What are the availability requirements of such storage	Highly available
Does any retention period apply?	Details not available
Are there any sources which does not have direct internet connectivity?	Details not available
What are source OS version (Windows/ Linux)?	Details not available
Does these resources support direct logging to the storage/analytical system?	Yes
Do these data need to be integrated with any other system?	No
Would you like to leverage Preview services?	Yes* (we are assuming yes to explore the latest services in preview). However, in most production scenarios, it is assumed mostly No.
Does the solution require it to be integrated with any of the existing SIEM system/Monitoring system/other management services?	Yes. This can be integrated with existing SCOM management group to utilize existing solution.

Monitor

Solution Scoping Questions	Responses Based on Available Data/ Suggested Solution
Do we need to monitor continuously?	
Which Metrics and Logs are required to be monitored? We have various options for the components we have. However, below are the ones we must monitor so that we can identify a failure and its cause if we need to. In certain scenarios, we may have to enable advanced monitoring for each of the components to diagnose and resolve a specific problem or failure. In our scenario, we can consider the below options for monitoring the use cases:	

1. Integrating existing SCOM infrastructure with Azure Monitor as explained earlier in this chapter (see the first section) so that all SCOM data are also ingested into Log analytics from on-premises servers and we have a single location with all the data and analysis.
2. All Azure application servers integrated to Azure Monitor VM insights streaming log and metrics data.
3. Application Insight containing all application logs.
4. SQL server analytics to monitor and report all SQL database-specific data logs.
5. Application Gateway analytics and diagnostic data to Log analytics.
6. Virtual network, VPN Gateway monitoring with Network watcher and endpoint monitoring with automated scripts to check on-premises to Azure connectivity.

Analyze

With the earlier monitoring setup and configurations in place, it would be more likely that we could identify a failure and also zoom into the details of the cause of failure. Most of the data will be analyzed by the solutions in use or can be analyzed manually. As you can see, there are three aspects to the monitoring strategy.

1. Monitoring a solution with regard to a specific scenario such as performance, availability, etc.;

2. Identifying the cause of such scenario; and

3. Reporting or informing the necessary contacts to take a necessary action (manual/automated).

Solution Scoping Questions	Responses Based on Available Data/Suggested Solution
Do you have specified thresholds to define alerts?	Not yet. We have assumed some standard values for discussion.
How do you want to Analyze the data? Manual/Log Search query/Alerts on Thresholds/Available Management solution integration/	Log Search, Management Solution, Alerts on events logged or metrics hit.
Who should be notified of such an event?	Collect the necessary e-mail addresses and phone numbers.
How should they be notified?	**E-mail** and **SMS**. Create an **Action Group** to trigger necessary contacts.
Any Automated actions to be taken?	Automated E-mail and SMS intimation for the necessary contacts.
Is there already an existing ITSM integration available for on-premises and/or Azure?	We will assume there is no existing ITSM integration in place with Azure Monitor.
Should the existing ITSM integration be used or can we suggest something else?	Yes.

Report and Visualize

Reporting, Visualizing, and Analyzing are interdependent. Granular visualization can lead to better analysis of data and identify any pattern. It can assist in identifying issues and indicate ways to resolve a problem. There are various ways to visualize the data available in Azure Monitor. Each of them provides different capabilities and advantages. You can choose whichever suits you better. Now, it's time for the question of the section: How do I choose a visualization tool? Well, there aren't any direct answers. Most organizations start with one and as they expand and requirements grow, they choose others over the existing ones. So, you will end up using more than one anyway at some point.

Solution Scoping Questions	Responses Based on Available Data/ Suggested Solution
What are your Reporting choices? Azure Dashboards/ Azure Monitor Views/ Workbooks/ Power BI/ Grafana/ Metrics Explorer	There aren't specific requirements of reporting mentioned. We can start with **Azure Dashboard** and **Azure Monitor views**. If required, we can explore other options.
Will there be an additional effort/ integration required for using such visualization tools?	None at this time. Unless advanced tools such as Grafana or PowerBI are required, we should be able to leverage Azure built-in tools for the visualization requirements.
Who should view or have access to such views/reports?	This is not clear and can be discussed with the customer.

Step 4: Ask Additional Questions or line down Your Assumptions

Additional Questions	Assumptions
Do you already have an existing Log Analytics workspace we should use?	We will have to create a new Workspace that will be used by all resources.
Do you already have an existing ITSM integration with Azure Monitor? What ITSM integration is required?	No. A new integration has to be created.
Who should view or have access to Monitoring views/reports other than the operational team e-mail id?	Everyone with the resource access or based on decided RBAC access at a later time.
What are the e-mail addresses and phone numbers of the necessary contacts for each of the items? Are there different groups for each resource? What are the common groups for various resources?	< as provided >
What are the access management requirements for the log's storage location?	Everyone with the resource access or based on decided RBAC access at a later time.
What are the access management requirements for the log's storage location?	Default permission unless otherwise required.
What are the availability requirements of such storage?	LRS by default. Log analytics and appinsight have their own availability.
Does any retention period apply?	We will assume default.

(continued)

Additional Questions	Assumptions
Are there any sources that do not have direct internet connectivity?	None.
What are source OS version (Windows/Linux)?	Both Windows and Linux.
Do these resources support direct logging to the storage/analytical system?	Yes
Do you have specified thresholds to define alerts?	We will assume based on Best practices.

Now that we have added the assumptions for the unknowns, we can work with these details to create the solution.

Step 5: High-Level Solution Detail

The objective of this section is to outline the solution configuration items so that we know what needs to be configured for each service and what the solution will look like.

Figure 5-24 depicts the high-level monitoring solution for our hybrid application environment.

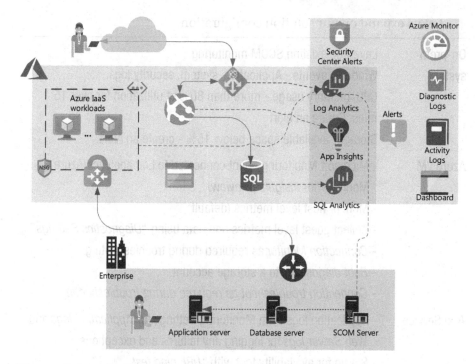

Figure 5-24. *C4cloud Application Monitoring high-level Solution diagram*

To monitor various components of the application:

- We have identified the core application components and dependencies through our solution approach.

- We analyzed why they should be monitored and how.

- We have also identified the various tools and configurations that are required.

- We have utilized all built-in Azure and existing on-premises tools wherever possible.

Let us expand on our solution configuration.

On-prem system	Leverage existing SCOM monitoring. Windows events - Application, system, security logs. CPU, memory usage - more than 80% of utilization for over 15 mins. Create an alert Storage- available space below 15% - create an Alert.
Azure VM	- Microsoft Monitoring agent connected to Log analytics/Azure Monitor with *Insights (Preview)* - Monitor host level metrics (default) - Collect guest level metrics and data using *"Diagnostics Settings"* - *Connection Monitor* as required during troubleshooting - *Boot diagnostics* to a storage account - *Connection troubleshoot as required during troubleshooting*
App Service	- Application logs from Monitoring Settings for *Application logs* and *Web Server logs* for logging any failures and exceptions - Set up for availability test with *"URL ping test"* *There are other ways to set up an Availability test as well including the "Multi-step web test" and "Custom track availability test." These require creating the Tests from Visual Studio and uploading to execute on the Azure portal. These are primarily used for advanced scenarios.* - *Monitor application for failures using Portal.*
SQL database	- Query performance insight - Azure SQL Analytics - Metrics and Diagnostics logging
Application gateway	- Application gateway Diagnostic Settings - Bac-End Pool health - Endpoint metrics

(continued)

Network connectivity	- Network Watcher - Virtual network diagnostic logs - Connection troubleshooter if required.
VPN Gateway	- Gateway connectivity status check - Gateway Metrics
Health of all resources	Azure Services health; Trigger alert if resource not healthy in the region
Others/Misc	Azure Status, Azure Monitor Status

We have already looked at the configuration of Virtual Machine, App service Application gateway, network metrics, and its monitoring, alerting details in Chapter 4 for most of the components. We are not drilling into the configuration step-by-step process of configuration here. In any case, we will now touch upon some other additional aspects and concepts specific to this scenario.

You can leverage Application Map to identify the end-to-end connectivity. This can be accessed from Application Insight. Here is an example output shown in Figure 5-25.

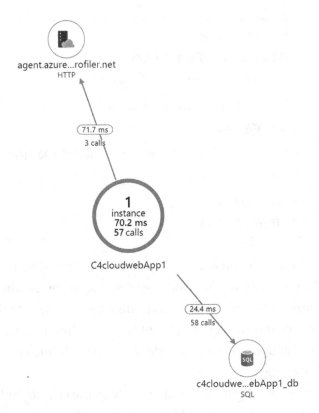

Figure 5-25. Application Map

Monitoring Application Availability

Application Service Availability with URL Ping Test

One of the easiest ways to identify if an application is accessible is by testing the application access itself. To do so in an automated way, a URL ping test can be used from Application Insight. A URL ping test uses advanced HTTP request-response mechanisms to check the application availability, response time, or performance associated and capability to add advanced custom validation criteria. For this you need to go to the Application Insight ➤ Investigate section ➤ Availability page, and then create a new test as shown in Figure 5-26.

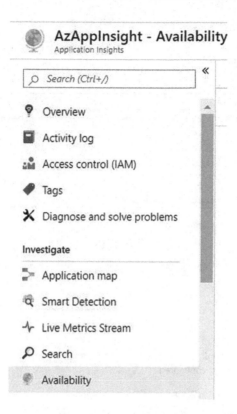

Figure 5-26. *Application Insight Availability monitoring*

You then provide the Application URL you wish to monitor and all possible locations from where your user base is located. These locations will be used for monitoring. You can choose a maximum of 5 locations. Also mention the HTTP response code you expect, for example, 200, and test the timeout period in seconds, etc. Figure 5-27 shows the create test page for availability testing.

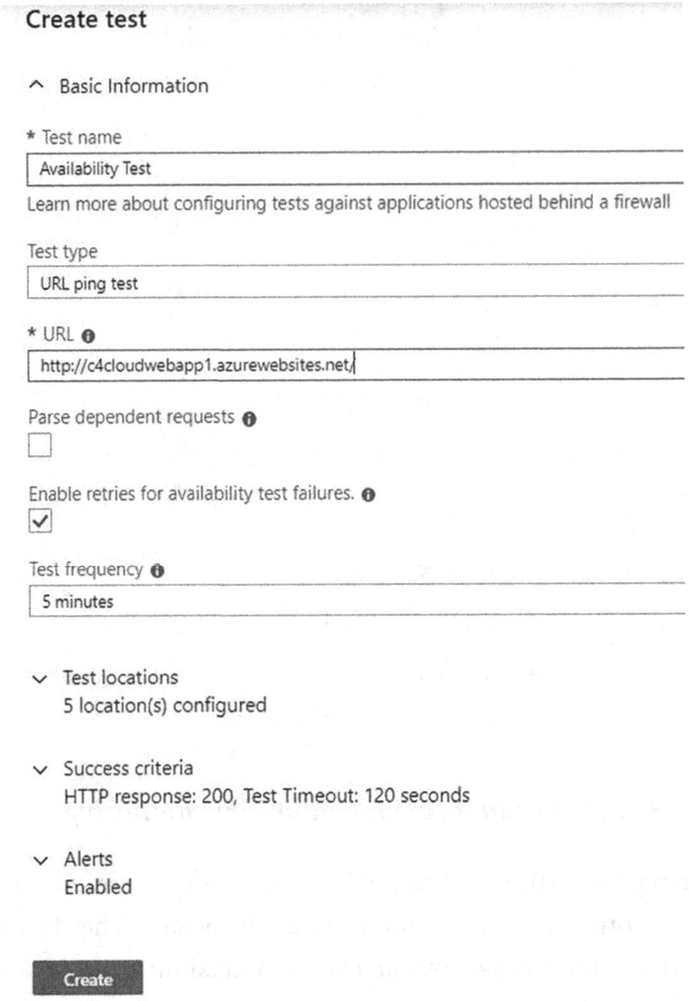

Create test

∧ Basic Information

* Test name

Availability Test

Learn more about configuring tests against applications hosted behind a firewall

Test type

URL ping test

* URL ❶

http://c4cloudwebapp1.azurewebsites.net/

Parse dependent requests ❶
☐

Enable retries for availability test failures. ❶
☑

Test frequency ❶

5 minutes

∨ Test locations
    5 location(s) configured

∨ Success criteria
    HTTP response: 200, Test Timeout: 120 seconds

∨ Alerts
    Enabled

Create

Figure 5-27. *Application insight availability test configuration*

The automated testing is done based on Test frequency. The minimum value you can specify here is 5 minutes. You show the overall count of success and failure and the failure region so that appropriate action can be taken for that location. Figure 5-28 is a sample output for such a monitoring.

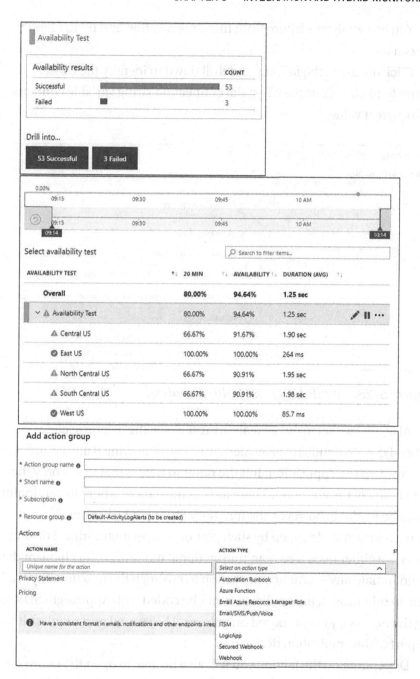

Figure 5-28. *Configuring Action groups*

You can analyze a failure from the same location and try to identify the cause.

Click on any of the failures and drill down to identify the cause. Figure 5-29 is an example when the connection string variable contains an incorrect value.

Figure 5-29. Availability test failure analysis

Also, we can set up an availability test to see the response code either 4xx or 5xx and create an alert, thereby identifying if any failure had occurred on the application. But the point to note is that this is only the availability of the endpoint. There are circumstances where the endpoint could be working; however, the functionality could be broken. Such scenarios cannot identified by such platform-level monitoring. For such cases, we either need a custom transactional monitoring mechanism that could initiate any synthetic transaction to ensure if the functionality is all fine. In other cases, the application can be coded with AppInsight SDK to log the necessary events based on failures. The second part requires it to be part of the application design and code.

Depending on the failure, you will also be able to open the entire stack in Visual Studio and track down to the point of failure.

So, are there other ways to monitor application availability in advanced scenarios? Yes, we can also create and upload a multistep scenario using Visual Studio and upload the scenario to be run in Application Insight. It executes the steps at regular intervals and records the response. Another way to achieve an advanced scenario is to use the TelemetryClient. TrackAvailability method in the code and report availability.

Application Gateway – Back-End Pool Health

Since the application is hosted behind an application gateway, the back-end health is another place that can show the health of the endpoint. The back-end health of the application gateway is based on the httpprobe defined by the rule. Figure 5-30 represents an unhealthy endpoint of an Application Gateway.

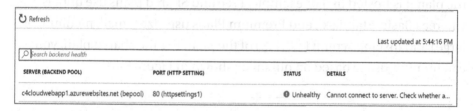

Figure 5-30. *Unhealthy Applcation Gateway back-end pool*

Application Gateway Endpoint Metrics

The same is also available in the metrics of the Application Gateway. *The Unhealthy Host Count* can be set up to trigger an alert if the value becomes a positive count.

Application Gateway Diagnostic Settings

An application gateway generates a huge amount of transactional-, access-, performance-, and health-specific data in the form of logs and data. These can be set up, using Monitoring blade in the App Gateway

Diagnostic Settings configuration. These logs and data can be routed to our Log Analytics workspace to be analyzed. The logs include **ApplicationGatewayAccessLog**, **ApplicationGatewayPerformanceLog**, **ApplicationGatewayFirewallLog**. For metrics, AllMetrics should be enabled to gather all necessary performance data.

Monitor Application Failures and Performance Logs for Application Services

You can enable logging either by Enabling Agents using the portal or manually instrumenting the application through code with Application Insight SDK.

Logs and metrics created by Application Service also depend on the plan it is hosted in. For example, Free and Shared plans use quotas whereas Basic, Standard, and Premium Plans use Size (small, medium, or large) and instance count (1,2,3 …) of the plan. For the shared plan, you can monitor usage based on quotas as shown in Figure 5-31.

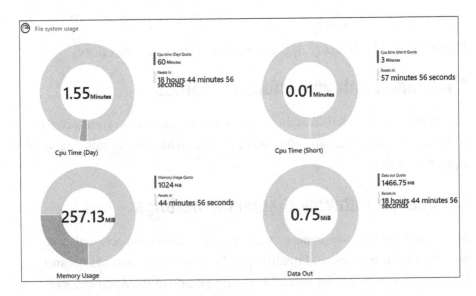

Figure 5-31. *App service Quota usage*

Failure Investigation Using Application Insight

Application Insight contains detailed information for all failures and exceptions for the application. You can drill based on Operations, Exceptions, Dependencies and Roles, or failure on the Server or browser. You can drill deeper into the event to identify what level of failure it encountered. A failure at the browser, server level, or any operational or code-level, failure, etc. Figures 5-32 and 5-33 help to visualize one such failure when the application did not return any response.

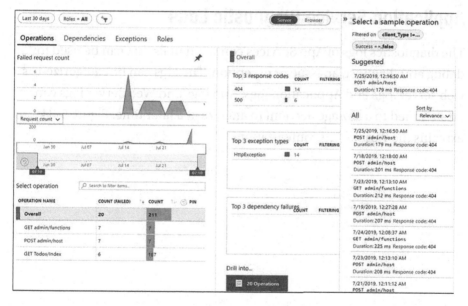

Figure 5-32. *Application failure analysis based on response code*

For errors, you can select the failures and open the sequence of events to identify what happened before or after the exact failures - **User flows**.

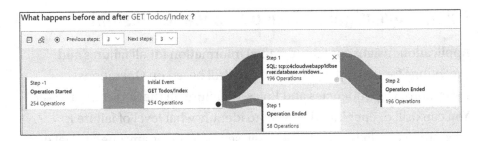

Figure 5-33. *Application failure analysis based on operational event before and after*

Application Service Diagnostic Logs

The diagnostics logs of App Services contain details that can be used to debug and diagnose an issue or exception. The logs can be categorized as web server logs and Application logs. App logs and Web Server logs can be streamed to a storage account to analyze at a later time. Figure 5-34 explains the various log configurations.

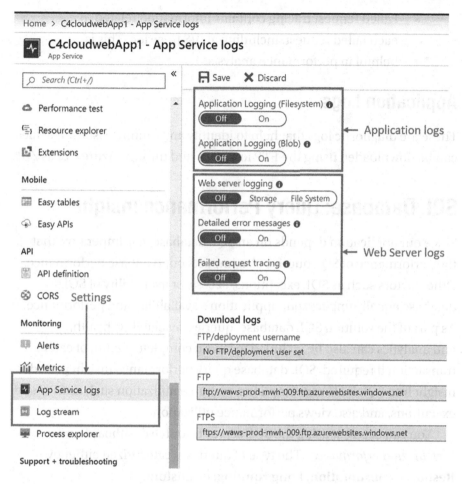

Figure 5-34.   Configuring Application Service Logs

Web Server Logs

Web Server logging contains, in overall HTTP transactions, site metrics details.

- This includes detailed error logging for 4xx and 5xx response codes. It created html files containing detailed information.

197

- Failed request tracing contains information related to each failed request, including an IIS trace log. This is helpful in performance analysis.

Application Logs

These are diagnostic logs that help to identify any runtime issues. The files can be downloaded using the FTP locations and through Azure CLI as ZIP.

SQL Database: Query Performance Insight

Since our application depends on an SQL database, it is imperative that the performance of SQL queries also impacts our database performance. Other factors such as SQL exceptions, access, or availability of SQL database equally impacts our application's availability and performance. As part of the solution SQL database, queries, availability, health, and analytics can also be included to have a complete picture of each transaction if required. SQL database query performance insight provides insight into SQL DTU consumptions, resource utilization such as CPU and executions, and also views performance utilization.

You can access it using the SQL server resource dashboard under *"Intelligent Performance."* The type of queries is categorized either by **Resource consumption, Long running,** or **Custom.**

You may also view the Performance overview and recommendations based on scenarios as shown in Figure 5-35.

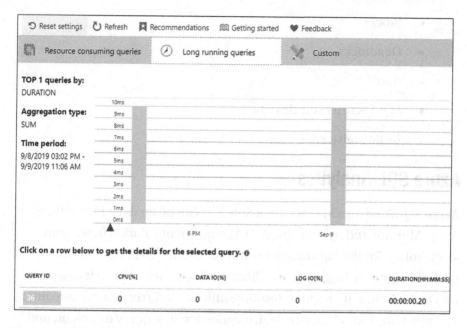

Figure 5-35. *SQL database query insight*

Metrics and Diagnostics Logging

The SQL server also generates relevant logs for analysis. It supports either
streaming to a storage account, Event Hub, or Log Analytics. The list of logs
includes the following:

- SQL Insights

- AutomaticTuning

- QueryStoreRuntimeStatistics

- QueryStoreWaitStatistics

- Errors

- DatabaseWaitStatistics

- Timeouts

199

- Blocks

- Deadlocks

- Audit

- SQLSecurityAuditEvents

- Basic Metrics

Azure SQL Analytics

Azure SQL Analytics Management Solution can be enabled from within Azure Monitor and by selecting Add Management solution from Azure Marketplace for the log analytics workspace. Once enabled, you can enable Diagnostic logging (to be discussed) to generate deeper insight into the Solution. It provides Resource utilization; Error/issues; timeouts; and Blocking issues based on SQL diagnostics logs, query durations, and automatic recommendations, just to name a few.

Figure 5-36 depicts the solution page once SQL Analytics is enabled using Management Solution in Azure Monitor.

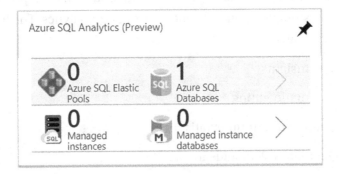

Figure 5-36. *SQL database analytics management solution*

Monitor for Virtual Network Service

Network is a core foundational service without which no solution, application, or environment is complete. For identifying any failure, performance, reliability, and availability issues, the network and its associated components such as gateways and devices are required to be monitored too.

Azure Monitor includes Network Watcher that enables you to do the following:

- Network monitoring with packet capture

- Deep insight into network traffic

- Analyze VPN connectivity issues

- VM communications and VPN network communication

- View various resource's relationship in a virtual network

It has a rich set of tools to identify any failures and issues, including VM to VM communication, routing and NSG traffic issues, and VPN troubleshooting. As shown in Figure 5-37, you can enable a network watcher for your region of deployment, for example, East US 2 from Azure Monitor ➤ Insights ➤ Network.

NAME	REGION	STATUS
	▼ 31 regions	Partially enabled
	West US	Disabled
	East US	Disabled
	North Europe	Disabled
	West Europe	Disabled
	East Asia	Disabled
	Southeast Asia	Disabled
	North Central US	Disabled
	South Central US	Disabled
	Central US	Disabled
	East US 2	Enabled

Figure 5-37. Enabling Network Watcher

Network Watcher includes *Network performance Monitoring,* which helps to do the following:

- Monitor network connectivity from Azure to on-premises including latency, path, health, and any other in-time or transient failures;

- Datacenters and various user locations;

- Application subnets containing various system and end-to-end connectivity;

- Expressroute circuits topology including Dynamics, Office365, and other network paths.

VPN connectivity can be troubleshooted and analyzed using Network Watcher. In addition, you can also use an automation script to check the health of the VPN gateway and trigger an alert in the event of any issues. In addition, we can monitor the VPN gateway for necessary bandwidth utilization, etc., using Azure Monitor Alerts.

There are lot of other ways and options that can be explored to achieve the various networking scenarios. In our case here, however, this should suffice.

Summary

With the details discussed so far, we have come to the end of this chapter. We looked at various integration scenarios with on-premises and Azure services, Azure tenant services (Azure Active Directory), Integration with on-premises SIEM systems, and a complete walkthrough of an application that has a presence on Azure and on-premises. In the example scenario, we tried to explore how to approach a solution with the set of requirements at hand: what questions to ask, how to approach, what additional details to gather, and how to identify what configurations could help achieve the objective. The scenario will work as a tool to understand the approach and break it down to create the solution. There will be additional questions depending on the scenario. However, we tried to cover the items that are common to a majority of the scenarios. Also, it should be easy to add new questions and identify a solution if we divide the architectural constructs as we did in this case.

CHAPTER 6

Continuous Monitoring and Changes

The constructs of monitoring keep evolving at a rapid pace, especially in cloud and hybrid architectures. It is important to remain updated about changes on the monitoring front to ensure that you are using the latest and greatest of the tools and services available at your disposal. With DevOps culture being absorbed in all aspects of IT management, monitoring cannot be far behind. This chapter will focus on the aspects on continuous monitoring and upcoming new features and changes in Azure monitoring.

Continuous Monitoring

In an environment where DevOps processes and tools are used for end-to-end deployment of infrastructure and applications, it is important to incorporate monitoring in all phases of the IT life cycle. This is often referred to as Continuous Monitoring aligned with the DevOps terminology of Continuous Integration and Continuous Deployment. The goal is to identify issues early on during the application life cycle and take necessary remedial actions.

© Bapi Chakraborty and Shijimol Ambi Karthikeyan 2019
B. Chakraborty and S. A. Karthikeyan, *Understanding Azure Monitoring*,
https://doi.org/10.1007/978-1-4842-5130-0_6

Full Stack Visibility

Azure Monitor can be integrated with your application from the initial phase of development through IDEs like Visual Studio and Visual Studio code. When the code is deployed, it can be used with DevOps tools to identify possible issues based on monitoring information. For ongoing maintenance and management after deployment, you could use the out-of-the-box monitoring features available through Azure Monitor or integrate it with your inhouse tools as discussed in Chapters 4 and 5 of this book. Full stack visibility of your business-critical applications can be achieved through components like Azure DevOps, Release pipeline integration with Azure monitoring, Application Insights, and Live Metrics. Figure 6-1 tries to draw the overall picture in this regard.

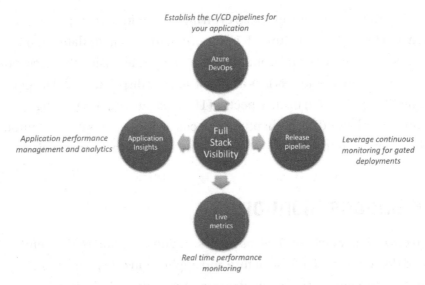

Figure 6-1. *Constructs of full scale visibility of continuous monitoring*

As the diagram depicts, the full stack visibility configuration is linked to the life cycle of the code starting from the repository it resides in that can be linked to Azure DevOps to create a continuous integration and delivery pipeline. Quality gates in the Azure DevOps pipelines enable monitoring of important health and performance metrics as the application is deployed across multiple environments. Additionally, Live Metrics and Application Insights take care of the monitoring once the application is deployed to Azure.

Continuous Deployment and Monitoring

Azure pipelines can be used for continuous deployment of both your code and applications. Monitoring can be integrated to your application release pipelines so that the collected data can be used for decision-making, that is, whether the code should be deployed to a target environment or if a rollback should be triggered.

- The template "Azure App Service deployment with continuous monitoring" available in Azure pipelines can be used to configure application insights for your App Service during deployment.

- The template has prebuilt alerts rules for the failed requests, service availability, server response times, and exceptions. These rules can be configured based on your requirements during pipeline setup.

- Pre-deployment and post-deployment gates can be configured to use "Query Azure Monitor alerts" so that you can access both Azure Monitor as well as Azure Application Insights alerts.

- Update evaluation option settings based on desired business logic. For example, you can set a timeout for the gate to fail based on the alert configuration.

- Post-configuration, you can review the release logs to gain insights on the behavior of the gates.

You can also use options like status monitor and live metrics to get real-time information on your application performance. For historical data, it is recommended that you leverage Application Insights. Application Insights can also be used to learn the application behavior over a period and fine-tune it accordingly. The key aspect is to identify the integration point for monitoring from which you get the information relevant to make right decisions.

Relevance of Infrastructure Monitoring

In previous chapters we covered the different ways to configure monitoring for your infrastructure. Here let us summarize what we have learned to reiterate the importance of monitoring infrastructure, which is the lifeblood of your applications.

- The metrics available by default would be your starting point to collect monitoring data. The relevant metrics should be identified and used to create alerts or pinned to Azure Dashboards for constant monitoring.

- Azure Monitor for VM or VM insights (Preview) offers additional information about health, performance, and automated dependency mapping. This feature gives a holistic view about your VM as well as its dependencies. Furthermore, the information is streamed to Log analytics and can be used to run custom queries to gainer deeper insights.

- Monitoring solutions in the Log analytics workspace can be used to gain better visibility into the status of your applications and virtual machines connected to your workspace. Solutions like Antimalware assessment, Azure activity logs, NSG analytics, and

AD health check are available out of the box, where information is represented in prebuilt graphs for instant visibility to the service status.

- Applications using microservices architecture through services like AKS, ACI, etc., can use Azure Monitor for containers as well as container monitoring solutions available in Log analytics to keep an eye on the health of a container-hosting infrastructure.

- Deployment of Infrastructure using the Infrastructure as Code approach will help you to incorporate monitoring components from day 1 of the deployment. This can be done using popular approaches like ARM template or Terraform via DevOps pipelines.

- Azure resource group monitor is a service that is in preview that can be used to get a bird's-eye view of dependent components in a resource group. You can view information on active alerts, health, and performance issues, etc., for all resources in your resource group using this service.

Continuous Changes

Microsoft Azure is an ever-evolving platform with over thousands of new features being released across various services each year. It is expected that some of the services, features, and options may change over period; get better; or even getting deprecated. Hence it is of the utmost importance to always review the Azure products by region (https://azure.microsoft. com/en-us/global-infrastructure/services/) website every time there is a new deployment. To that effect we will explore some of the latest and upcoming features in this chapter. Although these may change, no conversation is complete without looking at "What's new?" Let us now put this another way.

- If you do not want to use a "preview" feature for your production workloads and since you are unsure of how long it might take to be globally available (GA) as well, check the Azure products by region site for a region and its services. You may however, at times get a confirmation from the Azure product team if any of the public preview features are available with production support. This may help in considering the new service or feature to be included in the project or solution.

- Should you wish to keep a track of what is new and evaluate features for your solution and change the way it is currently configured, you may want to bookmark the Azure updates website: `https://azure.microsoft.com/en-us/updates/`.

Now let's look at some of the interesting enhancements.

Azure Monitor Status Blog

Monitor Azure Monitor using Azure Monitor status blog (Figure 6-2), if you are experiencing service issues, keeps you updated on the developments. The current URL is: `https://techcommunity.microsoft.com/t5/Azure-Monitor-Status/bg-p/AzureMonitorStatusBlog`. It not only provides ongoing issues and developments but also tries to suggest any workarounds that can be implemented by customers to provide relief.

Migrate from Classic Alerts Easily

The new Azure Monitor alerts are better with added granularity and multiple filter capability. You can also create a single rule that spans across multiple resources in various resource groups in one Azure region. This will help with the ease of rules management and quick deployment of alerts. All existing classic rules will be migrated by Microsoft starting in July 2019 if it has not already done so, using the tools provided to existing Azure customers.

Azure Monitor Now Supports Containers in China

Microsoft recently rolled out support for Azure Monitor for containers in Azure China. It provides end-to-end Kubernetes monitoring for AKS from infrastructure to workloads.

Identify Open or Bound Ports on Your Virtual Machines

This has always been a point of focus for security and operational teams from the security and troubleshooting aspects. With Azure Monitor you can now easily analyze which ports are open and active. The Microsoft Azure Monitor product team has also included an Azure VM workbook that includes active ports, failed connections, open ports, connections overview, traffic, etc. You can access this workbook once you enable the Insights (preview) monitoring from the Virtual machine settings pane. Once done, go to the Log analytics workspace, select Virtual Machines(preview) ➤ Map ➤ view workbooks. Figure 6-2 depicts the various network-related workbooks from Azure Monitor Virtual Machines Insights (preview).

Figure 6-2. Virtual machine workbook in Azure Monitor

Alternatively, you can use a Log analytics query and list the open ports. Here is a simple example to list the number of open ports. Figure 6-3 presents a chart of a sample query and the possible outputs.

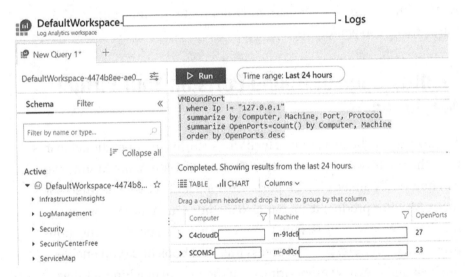

Figure 6-3. Log analytics query and output for Virtual machine open ports

Advanced Scoping with Additional Resources

Azure Monitor now includes advanced scoping for additional resources by embedding a "Logs" search from the resource menu. Users will not have to choose any specific Log analytics workspace, as all logs are automatically aggregated from various workspaces that include logs that are associated with the resource selected. Figure 6-4 represents the Log analytics workspace scoped to Virtual network. You can simply navigate to it by selecting the resources (Virtual Network in this case) and then Logs under the Monitoring section.

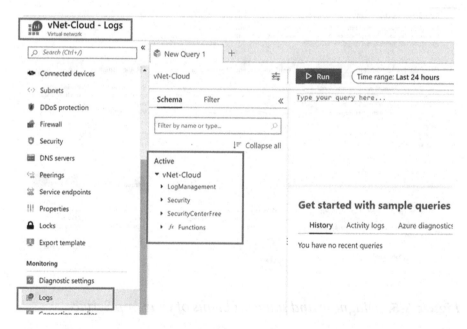

Figure 6-4. *Advanced scoping for Virtual Network*

However, for this to work, Access control mode of the workspace has to be set to "Use resource or workspace permissions."

Application Change Analysis with Azure Monitor

It is difficult to track and identify which changes cause a failure when multiple teams work together. App services *Diagnose and Solve Problems* now contains several traces and rules that can help you to identify a failure of the application, including IP configuration rule changes, incorrect connection strings, any binary modifications, or any web configuration file modifications. You can navigate by clicking on "Diagnose and solve problems" of your App Service as shown in Figure 6-5.

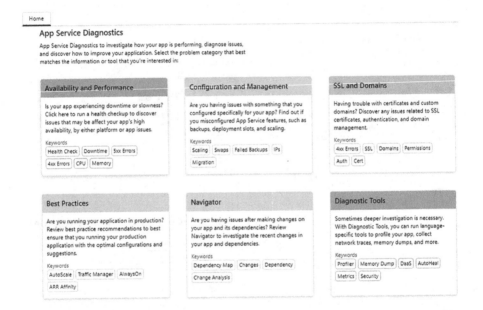

Figure 6-5. *Diagnose and solve problems of your App Service*

Figure 6-6 is an output of a failure where the client failed to access the website since it was restricted by a Networking rule in the App Service configuration.

Which client IPs got rejected due to IP restriction?

IP addresses rejected due to IP address restrictions configured on the app

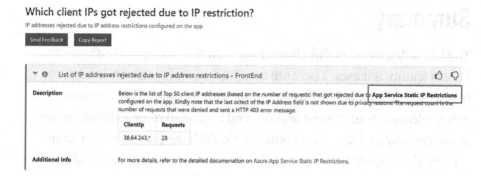

Send Feedback   Copy Report

✓ ⓘ List of IP addresses rejected due to IP address restrictions - FrontEnd	👍 👎

Description	Below is the list of Top 50 client IP addresses (based on the number of requests) that got rejected due to **App Service Static IP Restrictions** configured on the app. Kindly note that the last octet of the IP Address field is not shown due to privacy reasons. The request count is the number of requests that were denied and sent a HTTP 403 error message.

ClientIp	Requests
38.64.243.*	28

Additional Info	For more details, refer to the detailed documenation on Azure App Service Static IP Restrictions.

Figure 6-6. *App Service IP restriction in Diagnose and solve problems*

Similarly, you can identify various failure scenarios, including application changes or various HTTP 4xx errors, as depicted in Figure 6-7.

HTTP 4xx Errors

This view helps you identify all the HTTP 4XX requests for your app and provides insights on common solutions that you can take to further investigate and resolve these errors.

Send Feedback   Copy Report

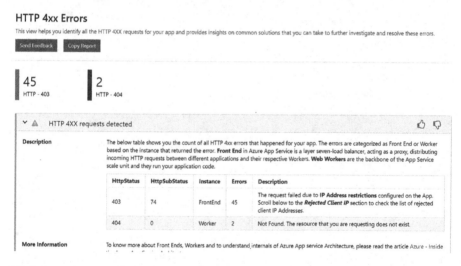

45	2
HTTP - 403	HTTP - 404

✓ ⚠ HTTP 4XX requests detected	👍 👎

Description	The below table shows you the count of all HTTP 4xx errors that happened for your app. The errors are categorized as Front End or Worker based on the instance that returned the error. **Front End** in Azure App Service is a layer seven-load balancer, acting as a proxy, distributing incoming HTTP requests between different applications and their respective Workers. **Web Workers** are the backbone of the App Service scale unit and they run your application code.

HttpStatus	HttpSubStatus	Instance	Errors	Description
403	74	FrontEnd	45	The request failed due to **IP Address restrictions** configured on the App. Scroll below to the ***Rejected Client IP*** section to check the list of rejected client IP Addresses.
404	0	Worker	2	Not Found. The resource that you are requesting does not exist.

More Information	To know more about Front Ends, Workers and to understand internals of Azure App service Architecture, please read the article Azure - Inside

Figure 6-7. *HTTP 4xx errors in Diagnostics and solve problems*

Summary

The items discussed in this chapter are merely a fraction of the vast flow of feature releases. There are continuous improvements in terms of new services supporting new regions, new features of the services being released in additional regions, and more and more capabilities are made globally available every other week. With the pace at which Azure is expanding its services and features, it opens up new scenarios of how a solution is designed, planned, and implemented. The same goes with Azure Monitor. In the coming days, expect to see several changes that make this scalable, multi-cloud, highly available, reliable monitoring platform even more agile and robust.

Index

A

© Bapi Chakraborty and Shijimol Ambi Karthikeyan 2019
B. Chakraborty and S. A. Karthikeyan, *Understanding Azure Monitoring*,
https://doi.org/10.1007/978-1-4842-5130-0

Printed in the United States
By Bookmasters